# NEO-SOLO:
## 131 NEO-FUTURIST SOLO PLAYS
## FROM
## TOO MUCH LIGHT MAKES THE BABY GO BLIND®

# Neo-Solo:
# 131 Neo-Futurist Solo Plays from
# Too Much Light Makes The Baby Go Blind®

*written by*

The Neo-Futurists:

Greg Allen

Dave Awl

Andy Bayiates

Sean Benjamin

Rachel Claff

Bill Coelius

Marjorie Fitzsimmons

Genevra Gallo

Ayun Halliday

Scott Hermes

Chloë Johnston

Connor Kalista

David Kodeski

Greg Kotis

Noelle Krimm

Anita Loomis

Steven Mosqueda

Rob Neill

John Pierson

Phil Ridarelli

Heather Riordan

Geryll Robinson

Stephanie Shaw

Diana Slickman

Lusia Strus

*edited by*

Diana Slickman

Hope And Nonthings

All inquiries concerning rights to any and all of the plays
contained herein should be addressed to:

Hope And Nonthings
PO Box 148010, Chicago, IL 60614-8010
773-528-5568 Fax: 773-529-4248
www.hopeandnonthings.com

Library of Congress Cataloging-in-Publication Data

Neo-Solo: 131 Neo-Futurist Solo Plays
from Too Much Light Makes The Baby Go Blind®

Contents: Short plays by members of The Neo-Futurists ensemble. Includes index.

I. Title  II. Monologues

[2002]

ISBN 0-9707458-8-5

Library of Congress Control Number: 2002110638

Edited by Diana Slickman
Designed by Louise E. Molnar
Published in the United States of America
First Edition 2002

The Neo-Futurists are an ensemble of writer/performer/directors founded in Chicago in 1988 by Greg Allen. The company's signature production is the late-night hit *Too Much Light Makes The Baby Go Blind*, an ever-changing attempt to perform thirty plays in sixty minutes, created by Greg and written and performed by the ensemble fifty weeks a year. In December of 2002, *Too Much Light* will mark 14 years of performance, making it Chicago's longest-running original show. In 1995, a second ensemble was formed and for two years produced *Too Much Light* in New York City. The Neo-Futurists also produce a full season of original full-length productions and tour the country (and a couple of cities outside the country) with *Too Much Light* and other productions.

# Table of Contents

## THE PLAYS

# Preface:
# Two Minutes of Original Material

In 1992, old enough to know better, I auditioned for *Too Much Light Makes The Baby Go Blind.* I did not know what I was getting myself into. All I knew was that I needed two minutes of original material to present at the audition. Which, luckily, I just happened to have. In fact, I had four minutes of original material. Anyone who has ever auditioned knows (or ought to, by god) that you don't exceed your allotted time. I had to edit. Half an hour before my audition I edited a minute and a half out of my piece. I memorized the shorter version, still thirty seconds too long, hoping momentum would take care of the difference. As I say, I was old enough to know better, but did it any how. My auditors were very kind, and let me finish the whole thing. It's still too long, that piece. It's on page 53; feel free to chop another minute out of it if you can.

There are other solo plays that were used for audition here. Stephanie sat on the floor of the theater and applied creme bleach to her upper lip in order to become a Neo-Futurist. Rob brought in his Bambi lamp for a poetic show and tell. A story about his Uncle Leonard was Steve's audition piece. For almost all of us in the ensemble, it was our first task, our ticket into the group, to write a short play for one person to perform. A monologue, a solo work. Two minutes on stage, alone, to reveal as much as we could about ourselves as writers, performers, people.

*Too Much Light* is an on-going, ever-changing attempt to perform thirty plays in sixty minutes. Each week the ensemble of writer/director/performers have to generate at least two to twelve new plays for the show, a number determined by the role of the dice. The plays can take any form that suits the author, with only a few restrictions: we cannot ask the audience to suspend their disbelief, we must be truthful, we must be economical with our time. The solo play is a staple dish on the *Too Much Light* menu. It can be argued that it embodies the Neo-Futurist aesthetic in its purest form: one person communicating an idea to a room full of other people without intermediary.

The plays in this collection were selected by the authors themselves, with various motives. Some honored audience favorites, like "Mr. Science Demonstrates Othello." Others chose plays that illustrate the range that can be achieved within the self-imposed limitations of the Neo-Futurist model, such as "Democracy InAction" or "I'm Going to Give This to The Guy Sleeping on the Bench Outside." Some submitted plays they hold dear for their own reasons or plays that document a response to particular time, or event, or mood, as "The Ghoul" or "Roadkill" do. The only criteria was that they had to be solo plays.

What is a solo play? It seems obvious, right? A play for one. But defining a solo play turns out to be more complicated. It is a play for one performer? A play for one voice? A play performed by one person without technical assistance or audience interaction? Yes. And yes. And no. And sometimes. In my arbitrary tyranny as the editor of this volume, my answer to this question ruled. Some of the plays here call for the assistance of other performers to wrangle flashlights, maneuver props, provide voices or noises. If a tyrant needs justify herself, I included these plays because I saw a way around these other performers. They could be (forgive me) replaced by a recording or a lighting cue or effective presetting of props. If you don't agree (and if you happen to be one of those auxiliary performers, you probably don't), remember that I am a tyrant, and like all tyrants, I deal harshly with dissenters.

People who care, as I do, about things like grammar and proper punctuation and correct usage, may well take exception to some of the grammar, punctuation and usage they find throughout the book. In having to choose between preserving the individual styles of expression of the authors and making sure we all used the comma in a uniformly correct manner, I went with the author's preference. The way we write reflects the way we talk, who we are, and the spirit of the time. Typing away in her glass house, the tyrant accedes to the will of the people.

In the Neo-Futurist tradition, these plays are presented in a random order. The titles were pulled from an envelope, one by one, by a man occupied with the Sunday paper and a cup of coffee. Any interesting juxtapositions are the work of chance and caffeine, not any design of mine.

I could go on, but I'm about three minutes over my allotted time. I'm old enough to know better but still counting on momentum and a tolerant audience if I go a little long.

D. S.

# She Stands on the Lip: About Where We Work

To clarify some of the stage directions in the plays, a word or two should be said about the configuration of the playing spaces in which we have worked for so long.

On Valentine's Day, 1992, the company opened The Neo-Futurarium in a Swedish sororal organization's former headquarters and meeting hall above a funeral home in Chicago's Andersonville neighborhood. The stage is a wide, shallow, three-quarter thrust, with what might grandiosely be called "arena" seating. It is a long rectangular room with risers built along the short sides and one long side, and the floor is the stage. Behind the fourth and final row of seats in the center and left sections of the house are windows which open onto a breezeway and an alley, respectively. On temperate evenings we open the windows over the alley and occasionally our plays are interrupted or improved by shouts from passers-by or the toot of a car horn or the smell of calamari deep-frying at the Italian restaurant across the way. The tech booth and tech person (single-handedly responsible for all the light and sound in the show) are easily visible to the audience, house left. The door through which the audience enters is set into the upstage wall, far stage right. Our green room and prop room are off stage left. A low, wide step runs along the length of the upstage wall; we call it "the lip". Our lobby, a.k.a. the State Park, is on the other side of the upstage wall. Hanging from the lighting grid over the stage is a clothesline to which numbered pieces of paper representing the plays are pinned. A person standing on a regular household ladder can easily touch the ceiling above the grid.

Todo Con Nada, the basement theater which housed the New York production of *Too Much Light* during its second year has, as arguably its most remarkable feature, a door in the upstage wall of the playing space that opens directly on to Ludlow Street. The New York ensemble (Rachelle Anthes, Bill Coelius, Ayun Halliday, Spencer Kayden, Greg Kotis and Rob Neill) employed the sidewalk outside the door as an adjunct playing space and sometimes engaged passers-by for walk-on parts. The proximity of the stage to the street might be considered a liability to a "straight" theater. It was delicious grist for the mighty NY NF mill.

You may find any of these places and things referred to in the plays here, for we try to get the most out of our environment, its features and limitations. If you find a stage direction that says a play takes place under the risers, it is not a typo or a euphemism; the play is to be performed under the audience. How you might stage that in your theater is your problem.

# jack

*[Andy stands center behind a large podium. No tech. There is a small, plain, closed cardboard box on top of the podium.]*

**ANDY:**

Let's say that inside this box is something funny. If I were to open it, you would all laugh. It would be as easy as simply lifting this lid, and letting the contents out. Here is my hand. Here is the box. There you are, watching me. Waiting for me to lift the lid.

*[Pause]* I will not lift the lid, although every instinct I have is urging me to rip this box open and dump its contents all over the stage right now. And some of you are convinced that this play will end that way. But I assure you, during this play, I will not allow myself to open the box.

At this point, while I was writing this piece, I froze for a while. Because whenever I get close to this place, that is, imagining myself exposed in front of all of you with this box closed, I get scared.

*[Looks at box.]* I've witnessed a lot of ugly things in my life. I've lost a lot of people I can't forget, and lately I think one of the hardest things in the world is just having a conversation with someone...about anything.

And then every weekend there's all of you. And me. And this box. Up until now that particular relationship has been very functional. As far as what function that relationship serves in my life...I wouldn't have written this play if I didn't think I needed to.

*[Andy exits, leaving the box behind him.]*

CURTAIN

# Karen Finley Goes to Washington

© 1998 Rachel Claff

*[A podium on stage with a bottle of chocolate syrup on it, in a spotlight. Rachel is on a voiceover microphone. The text is spoken very quickly, almost as one sentence.]*

**RACHEL:**

In this dream I have never had but hope to have someday Karen is standing in a huge courtroom in front of a huge fat judge with a huge golden gavel. The fat judge is telling her that she is going to prison for doing indecent things with drippy foods and she is just about to say something when the back wall of the courtroom collapses and there's President Clinton sitting in his little chair being interrogated by Kenneth Starr's grand jury in the Map Room of the White House and he's sweaty and pale like the underside of a fish and when he sees Karen he starts making this weird little noise like choking but weirder than that. Karen looks at him for a long time while he keeps making the noise and then she strips down to a red, white and blue bikini and kneels in front of him and unzips him in front of the judge and jury and Dan Rather and Diane Sawyer and Sam Donaldson and Regis and Kathie Lee and Jerry Springer. And while everyone's watching and the cameras are rolling she sucks him off and sucks him off until her cheeks are full of semen like a chipmunk, like two big water balloons, and Diane Sawyer goes to Jerry Springer, "Do you think she spits or swallows?" and Jerry Springer just shrugs and keeps watching. But Karen doesn't spit and Karen doesn't swallow, she just turns around and suddenly Hillary Clinton is standing there in a see-through nightie, and Monica's there too except she's buried up to her neck in a chunk of concrete, and while everyone's watching Karen pulls Hillary's nightie up over her head and whoosh! She spreads Hillary's legs and spits the spunk right into her and wipes her mouth with her bikini top. And while everyone's watching Hillary Clinton's stomach starts to swell up and ploop! She gives birth to Jesse Helms full grown in a Brooks Brothers suit. And Jesse looks at Karen and Karen looks at Monica and Monica looks at Bill and Bill looks at the cameras and then Jesse Helms just starts laughing hysterically and nodding his head up and down and back and forth because he finally gets it, he finally completely gets it, and he gives Karen Finley a big fat kiss on her spermy wet mouth and while everyone's watching and the cameras are rolling the judge's golden gavel comes down hard like the end of the motherfucking world.

CURTAIN

# Branded

*[This is a very simple song, played on the guitar. Genevra may or may not ask for the audience to participate in the chorus.]*

**GENEVRA:**
Some time last year
I'm having dinner with my Dad.
And he says, "My dear,
it's clear that you're in love,
and for that I am glad.
But we should have seen you
walking down the wedding aisle by now."
And then he utters this insulting metaphor
in which I am a cow:

*Chorus:*
Why buy
Why buy
Why buy the cow when you can get the milk for free?

And then my Mom
sends me an email the other day,
"Nothing new here, honey,
but there's something I feel I have to say.
I think you need to leave
if you don't soon receive a ring."
And even though she's using different words,
she's still saying the same damn thing:

Why buy
Why buy
Why buy the cow when you can get the milk for free?

My grandmother's getting older,
slowing down, and passing 83.
Every time we talk she says she needs
to know he'll take care of me
when she's gone. And I think maybe they're right
and I am wrong.
So I spend two silly hours
making up this really stupid song:

Why buy
Why buy
Why buy the cow when you can get the milk for free?

[*Repeat chorus as needed.*]

CURTAIN

# Love, Honor and Obey

**SCOTT:**

Goddamn, my wife makes me feel sexy.

Now, I don't know how I look to you, you may not even be attracted to men period and you may think I look like some kind of freak, thing that crawled out from under a rock, well maybe if you were the last man on earth, but goddamn, my wife makes me feel sexy.

Look, I don't know what's wrong with her. Why when she looks at me, she gets that look, yes, that look, "you've got the look, you've got the look of love"—sexy, dammit. I don't know why this particular combination of eyes ears nose lips teeth smile chin legs butt dick back chest arms tongue gut neck make her loop the loop, but it does. And when she says c'mere, you bet your ass, your bottom dollar, your goddamn farm, and the motherfucking moon, that I drop what I am doing and run, jump, skip to my lou, my darling, my Clementine, my baby, baby, baby, baby, baby, baby please.

[*Beat*]

Goddamn, my wife makes me feel sexy.

CURTAIN

# Wite

[*Phil sits at table with a glass bowl partially full of milk; sugar; salt; a small boiled potato; whipped cream; a blank piece of paper; an eggshell (which has been hollowed out); and a white carnation. Phil performs the various actions throughout.*]

**VOICE OVER:**

Add two tablespoons of sugar to 1 cup of milk. Let this dissolve while you're at work. Try not to think about the sweet mixture sitting alone in your kitchen being stared at by the cat.

When you arrive home sob uncontrollably into your pillow case and let stand for 3 weeks. Add the salt that remains on the linens to the milk.

While you sit in silence in front of the TV, make a hat of whipped cream on a potato you've peeled with your teeth. Stare at it and think of the little men that used to move the furniture around when you closed your eyes at night. Add this little man to the mixture.

Gently fold a piece of paper.

Beat yourself up about the mistakes you've made. [*The eggshell is cracked. It is empty.*]

Add 2 cups flower. [*A white carnation is added.*]

Bake at 350 degrees and then rip out your heart. [*A peeled hard-boiled egg emerges from Phil's mouth.*]

CURTAIN

# The Buddha Receiving a Gift of Heart-Shaped Chocolates

© 1989 Dave Awl

[*Dave sits in a chair center stage and delivers the following poem directly to the audience:*]

**DAVE:**
You know very little about me now.
Not that I have a temper, for the first time in my life;
not the white shirt and tie I'm forced to put on every day,
or the way I carry twelve pounds of books in a backpack
on the off chance of getting five minutes to
read. You don't know of the dashing Ethiopian girl who
stole my hand to dinner last night, flashing an impossibly
English grin over huge plates of spongy bread and fava beans,
telling me about paraplegics and the history of a family
older than either of our troubles. You don't know that I
speak a bit of Spanish now, or that last night Gustavo
the dishwasher and I carried out the restaurant's garbage
together, and looked together for the evening moon,
and he told me that there was no moon,
*"estrelles solamente"*— stars only—
and I understood him. And he patted my back and we walked in,
shaking our heads at the moon's desertion. You'll never know
of my first kiss taken in danger on a rooftop, or what my
apartment looks like with the lights turned low and an
Edith Piaf tape playing, or how I found myself after many
years of distraction in a series of science fiction novels.
Most of all, you don't know that I haven't loved you almost
a year now, and no longer make jokes when your name comes up.
I know now that you'll know nothing about me ever again;
until perhaps we should meet again in the space
where these lives end, and events become meaningless
as they were always intended
to be.

CURTAIN

# LIAR

[*Bill stands center stage and during the delivery of text, wraps each body part mentioned in electrical tape.*]

**BILL:**

As he nodded YES, his toes turned in on themselves, his soft nails covering the baby hair, like a preserves lid. And as he nodded YES, his knobby feet were sucked up into his ankles with a motion so subtle, he at first felt he was standing in a pool of cooled maple syrup. And as he nodded YES, his knees, chapped and barbed, already in his hips, tickled his pelvis and he smiled,

"It's funny, not to have a leg to stand on."

And as he nodded YES, his pencil slipped away from his receding fingers, which wet his elbows with a disparaging gasp, his elbows then disappearing into shoulders like a sparrow into a cherry red bird box. And as he nodded YES, his head, sitting on his collar bone like a retreating sunset, slowly escaped into the awaiting calcium horizon...Skull, scalp, lips, teeth,...yes.

CURTAIN

# This Is Still Not a Pool

[*During the course of the play Diana strips down to a bathing suit and puts on swim goggles, lies on the floor and flails, as though swimming.*]

**DIANA:**

I am not very graceful. My form is poor. Even my breathing is difficult to coordinate, which makes it just about impossible for me to swim freestyle. But I can breast stroke well and side stroke like a maniac and though my backstroke is clunky, it lets me breathe whenever I want so I do that. The point is to keep moving, to keep moving and to think as little as possible. My body held aloft by water so chlorinated that the scent of it nearly makes me choke, I try to disconnect my mind so that it too can float, more or less gracefully, on the water.

I am a self-taught swimmer. Though I nearly drowned at least twice as a child, I never hesitated to get into the water and paddle around until, even on the hottest days, I was water-logged, blue-lipped, shivering. I love the water. I like to think it loves me, though I know it to be indifferent and impassive, not my friend, possibly a foe, a medium for death by drowning. The quiet below the surface is so complicated and inviting that it is easy to understand the suicide who wades out of her depth and lets the water pull her down. It's nice under there, under the water. Calm. Weightless. Peaceful.

[*She stops "swimming" and just lies there on her stomach. After a bit, she pushes her goggles up, squints along the floor.*]

Jesus Christ. You should see how much dirt there is on this floor.

CURTAIN

# DOMINATRIX AEROBIX INSTRUCTRIX

© 1993 Lusia Strus

**LUSIA:**

Alright, People! We'll have three seconds of warm-ups followed by a hundred and seventy-five minutes of high-impact aerobix. And that's aerobix with an [*she makes a whip sound*] X! Ready?

And Go! [*She begins aerobicizing.*] You made those thighs people. You make 'em go away. Genetics has nothing to do with it. Pain! Pain! It's all about pain! Just do it! What ever it takes! Just do it! One—two—get rid of that fat. Three—four—get me some ipecac! Yes!

[*Holds her hand straight above her head with her index finger extended. Whip sound.*] What is this? This is your numero uno tool! And tool to the throat and tool to the throat and tool to the throat and BEND! Again! Tool to the throat and tool to the throat and tool to the throat and bend! Yes!! It's all about feeling inferior! To get better you must believe that you are shit now! Disregard anything you have ever accomplished, people! You still have cellulite. Control yourselves! Control everything! It's all a matter of Will [*whip sound*] Power! And if someone doesn't love you because of your misshapen body, it is not their issue. It is YOUR PROBLEM! So! Who do you look to for inspiration? Oprah Winfrey, my hard ass! Think you get guns like these by celebrating your sissy bitch spirit?!

NO! Tori Spelling! Look to Tori Spelling for guidance! Her head is bigger than her torso, for God's sake! She must be doing something right!

[*Addressing an audience member.*] What are you smiling about? Here for yourself? For your own personal, physical, spiritual and emotional health? I know your kind. You'll never reach the weight on your driver's license with that attitude! I'll bet you read his horoscope in the *Trib* this morning, didn't you?! You're not over him yet!! Down, down, down like a dog. [*Lusia gets down on all fours and begins doing leg lifts.*] Get thin for him. No.

Get thin for Tori. Get thin for Tori. Just do it! [*Continuing leg lifts.*]

CURTAIN

[*Optional ending: After the last line above, the following exchange takes place:*]

**HEATHER:**
[*Entering.*] Lusia, what are you doing?

**LUSIA:**
[*Exhausted.*] Trying to get motivated.

CURTAIN

# Bad Haiku

© 2000 Greg Kotis

*[Greg stands before the audience to deliver the following bad haiku.]*

**GREG:**
White clouds cloak blue skies
A bird cries out to the sun
Because it was startled, one second the sun's behind the clouds the
       next it's not, it can get confusing for a bird...
       which are stupid animals anyway.

CURTAIN

# Drop It

*[The cast stands on stage in a tight group, center, gazing up at the ceiling. Rachel is amongst them. She addresses the audience.]*

**RACHEL:**

I hate New Year's Eve. What a miserable excuse for a holiday. Okay, sure, it's great if you actually have a *date* to celebrate with, but for the rest of the world, including me, it's go to the stupid party, get drunk, watch Dick Clark and a bunch of candy-coated pop singers counting down in Times Square where a whole bunch of people jammed together even drunker than you are honk annoying little horns and sing an incomprehensible song written in a language that's older than God.

*[The cast "la-la-la's" the beginning of "Auld Lang Syne," inventing words and generally being rowdy, and then stops suddenly.]*

Sure, you could call me bitter. Yeah, okay, I'm a little bitter. But honestly —I don't think it's being single or dateless or even the booze that gets me depressed. Know what it is? That goddamned ball drop. *Descending* on us, inch by inch, all lit up with promises we didn't keep, places we didn't go, people we didn't call, the resolutions that stayed unresolved all year long and now the year's over, last chance, whoops, too late. Three, two, one, *crunch*. Happy New Year.

The thing is, it should go up.

The ball. It should go up. It should start to rise, very slowly at first, and then just—go, sailing higher and higher until it's barely visible, just a glimmer, a star, a tiny little reminder. No countdown, just—

*[Everyone gasps and holds onto each other, still looking up.]*

And everyone holds their breath and follows it with their eyes, really quiet. And when it finally disappears, we all stop looking at the night sky and come back to each other and stare at each other in total amazement. Like we're seeing each other for the first time.

That's how it should be, I think.

*[Everyone slowly looks around at each other and the audience as the lights fade to black.]*

CURTAIN

# In That Smooth Silence

[*Steve speaks over the loud sound of a vacuum cleaner he is holding.*]

**STEVE:**
I go back and forth about what the first memory is I ever had, but I'm pretty sure it's of my mother doing housework and singing. She sang along to the hits of the day, Dionne Warwick/Burt Bacharach hits, The Carpenters, and The Fifth Dimension, but the one I remember the most is Peggy Lee singing "Is That All There Is." My mother had a great voice, soft and light, with a little sadness mixed in for texture. Besides picking up after four kids and a husband, there was the dusting and the laundry and the cooking. And I can still see her dancing with that loud heavy vacuum cleaner around the house, steering it in and out of the spaces between the furniture. And each time she'd run out of cord and had to plug it into another outlet, that's when I'd notice her singing the most, in that smooth silence. It was so beautiful I remember wondering if my mother was really a movie star and she just never told us about it. I didn't really know what the song meant at the time but over the years, when I listened more closely, the words and the memories collided in my mind and I felt so sorry for her. My mother lives alone now, still doing the dusting and the laundry and pushing a vacuum cleaner around the house. But now that I'm in my middle thirties, about the same age as she was back then, and I'm dancing around my small apartment, with my loud, heavy vacuum cleaner, I can't help but feel closer to her than I ever have.

[*The vacuum cleaner is shut off as we hear "Is That All There Is" by Peggy Lee.*]

CURTAIN

# Mr. Science Demonstrates Othello

© 1989 Greg Allen

[*Greg stands on stage behind a table which contains the following items: an Oreo cookie, a glass of milk, a white candle in a brass candle holder, a box of blue-tip matches, a bottle of rum, a box of animal crackers, a sticker with a smiley face on it, and a spoon. He uses these items in lecture/demonstration format to deliver the following speech. Lines and actions are placed side by side to more clearly indicate simultaneous activities.*]

**GREG:**

| | |
|---|---|
| Othello. | *Greg presents the Oreo cookie to the audience.* |
| Desdemona. | *Greg presents the unlit candle in its holder to the audience.* |
| Cassio. | *Greg presents the glass of milk.* |
| And I am Iago. | *Greg gestures to himself.* |
| Othello loves Desdemona. | *Greg lights the candle.* |
| Desdemona loves Othello. | *Greg holds the candle and the Oreo up together.* |
| It's an odd couple, but somehow it works. | *He puts them back down on the table.* |
| The story so far: Othello has passed over his good friend Iago for a medal and a promotion... | *Greg picks up the Oreo and waves it past himself.* |
| and, instead, has given it to Cassio. | *Greg puts the smiley face sticker on the glass of milk.* |
| Iago vows vengeance. | *Greg holds the spoon threateningly.* |
| Iago finds Cassio alone one day... | *Greg picks up the milk...* |
| gets him drunk... | *...pours rum into the milk and stirs it with a spoon.* |
| and manages to get him to kill off a rather minor character. | *Greg reaches into the box of animal crackers and takes one out randomly.* |
| In this case, a hippo. | *Greg throws the animal cracker into the milk.* |

Othello arrives upon the scene,
finds Cassio drunk over the dead body,…

*Greg picks up the Oreo and holds it over the glass of milk,…*

and immediately demotes Cassio,
and gives his promotion to Iago.

*takes the sticker off of the milk and sticks it on his shirt.*

This pleases Iago,

*Greg smiles.*

but he is not content.

*He stops smiling.*

Iago takes Othello aside one day…

*Greg picks up the Oreo…*

opens him up to what he has to say…

*twists the Oreo apart…*

and plants within him the notion,
the idea really,…

*and, using the spoon, scrapes out the middle of the Oreo,…*

that perhaps Desdemona and
Cassio are fucking around.

*and then mushes the white stuffing between his fingers.*

Othello pulls himself
back together…

*Greg puts the stuffing back in between the two Oreo halves…*

but he is never
quite the same again.

*and holds up the rather odd-looking, reconfigured Oreo.*

Meanwhile, the distraught Cassio
goes to his friend Desdemona to try
to get her to convince Othello into
giving him back his promotion.

*Greg puts the milk and the candle next to each other.*

This, of course, is witnessed by
the now jealous Othello, who
gets a little heated up about the
whole thing,…

*Greg holds the Oreo over the flame.*

and this foretells…

*Greg takes the candle out of its holder and lays the candle horizontally across it.*

Desdemona's…

*He then lights the other end of the candle so it now…*

ultimate…extinction.

*continues to burn at both ends.*

Othello is now spinning under

*Greg flips the Oreo cookie*

Iago's control...

and he actually asks Iago to do away with Cassio altogether.

Iago attempts...

but fails.

Finally, the horribly distraught Othello goes to Desdemona's bedchamber, and...

puts out the light...

and then...puts out the light.

Everyone then comes in and finds the now crumbling Othello over the extinguished body of Desdemona, and they tell him, that, of course, Desdemona was completely innocent and Iago had manipulated the whole thing. Just before Othello kills himself, Iago is dragged in to say his final line in the play which is "From this time forth, I never will speak word."

*into the air like a coin.*

*Greg picks up the rum, milk and cookie mixture.*

*Greg tries to drink the entire contents of the glass...*

*but cannot. He puts the glass back on the table.*

*Greg picks up the Oreo, separates the halves near the candle, and...*

*uses them to snuff out one end of the candle...*

*and then the other.*

*Greg eats the Oreo cookie and chases it with the glass of milk.*

CURTAIN

[*NOTE: Although "a hippo" is quite funny, the name of the actual animal should be substituted. If the "execution" of Desdemona proves difficult, the line "she struggles" may be added.*]

# A Simple Tale of Love

**GERYLL:**

There once was a woman who took up a great deal of space in my life. She had very sweet breath. Against all prior warnings and advice I sought her out and I loved her—this woman with the sweet breath—I loved her so much that I actually tried to give myself to her like a present or a gift.

One afternoon in her bed she played for me an album by a soulful sister named Joan and I clung to her moist body and cried into the sweet soft place where her neck and shoulder met. And it was at this moment that I knew that I would love this woman with the sweet breath that I would love her forever—for the rest of my life—forever.

And then something went wrong. Some irreversibly wrong and hateful element was sent to destroy. It traveled through her veins carrying the far off rhythms of a distant land that never existed.

Her breath became sour.

Her passion for me was slowly displaced by her obsession with this force in her veins, her lungs, her mind, her body—but her soul I often wonder...was it too infiltrated by this chemical destroyer? Or does her soul know that I love her still—the woman with the sweet breath—does her soul know that I'm sorry...I never got to say "goodbye"?

Goodbye.

CURTAIN

# One Night

[*Bill is sitting on stage in darkness. Behind him, a pair of trousers is illuminated.*]

**BILL:**

One night, I found my father beating a brush fire the size of a picnic table with his pants. With his fingers hooked into his belt loops for support he was frantically beating the fire which grew from the natural wheat separating us from our neighbors, the Radants, who of which, Phil, Judy, Stephen and Michael had congregated to join me and my brother in watching the strange flag codes my father was sending to invisible ships with his dirty, wool trousers. His stark white legs moving up into his underwear created the image of a large, shimmering tooth against the black Michigan sky. The tooth was screaming:

"DON'T CALL THE FIRE DEPARTMENT! DON'T CALL THE FIRE DEPARTMENT!"

For in the quickness and confusion of this low budget catastrophe, my father had not forgotten that the origin of this whole mess, an M-80 purchased in Indiana on a weekend whim, was very much illegal in the state of Michigan.

I think of my father's plight when I read newspaper articles about guilt and redemption: Mr. Simpson, Mr. Clinton and his Whitewater affairs, former Italian premier Burlusconi. And I think sometimes, justice flames and never goes away, and then sometimes I think escape is as easy as taking off your pants.

CURTAIN

# Profession of Faith

© 2000 Diana Slickman

[*The staging for this is hard to describe, but here goes: while speaking, Diana places three lengths of rope, coiled, on to the stage. Each rope is a different length and has slip knots at both ends. One at a time, she attaches the ropes to people in the audience. Without communicating with them about this in words, she slips the loop of the slip knot over the wrist of the audience member, tightens it up a little and then gets them to hold the long end of the rope in their hand. The other end of the rope is attached to a different person in the audience. The people attached to either end of a rope are equidistant from the center of the rope. Once the ropes are in place, Diana slips the center of each rope around her waist so that she is, in effect, the meeting point for three arcs of rope.*

*The delivery of the text is meant to be non-stop, but not rushed. The text and the task should take just about the same amount of time.*]

**DIANA:**

I believe in the invisible thread that binds us together.

I believe that when you go I go.

I believe that thinking makes it so.

I believe that when your ears burn someone is talking about you.

I believe in the intercession of saints.

I believe the intercession of saints is like a relay race where the baton of my prayer is passed from St. Jude to St. Catherine to St. Teresa to St. Bernadette to the BVM to Jesus until it crosses the finish line that is the very ear of God himself where it is answered in God's own mysterious language.

I believe it is no coincidence that actors and secretaries have the same patron saint.

I believe that no good deed goes unpunished.

I believe in civility toward everyone, no matter how loathsome.

I believe that when I think of you the phone rings.

I believe in miracles since you came along, you sexy thing, sexy thing you.

I believe that you should never carry a credit card balance because those motherfuckers don't deserve a single red cent.

I believe the worst of everyone and everything and I'm always surprised to be right.

I believe you love me still.

I believe I will never be older than 23 in my mind.

I believe that lack of love can kill you.

I believe that touch can heal.

I believe you.

I believe that there is no god.

I believe that death is nothing more mysterious than the transmutation of energy from one form to another.

I believe that if we were meant to be able to talk on the phone every-goddamned-where we'd have been born with receivers embedded into our palms.

I believe that there are no enterprises any more but the marketing and sale of goods and services of limited use and dubious value.

I believe that living well is the best revenge.

I believe that virtue is its own reward.

I believe the South will rise again.

I believe that there is a link that binds all people together and I don't mean some six degrees of separation celebrity match game bullshit so you can put that right out of your mind.

I believe that haste makes waste.

I believe that kindness begets kindness.

I believe that words beget words.

I believe that belief without action is meaningless.

I believe that we hold the thread of one another's lives in one hand and a pair of scissors in the other.

[*By this time Diana is standing on stage with the three ropes around her waist. At the end of the last line, she falls backward into the ropes, pulling them taut, requiring the lassoed audience members to hold tight in order to keep her upright (and to keep from being yanked out of their chairs.)* ]

CURTAIN


[*NOTE: How and if this visual works depends on how the audience and playing space are configured. Getting the tension, the angle of the fall, and the right distance between and among ropes take a little practice, and should be given a test run before trying it on an actual audience. It helps to figure out in rehearsal where you want the center of the arcs to be and then work backward from there. The people you chose to attach to the ropes can be in different rows of seats, sitting or standing. It will be up to you how to create the stage picture.*

*If you choose to do this play yourself, employ the form but change the content, and write a list of your own beliefs. If you believe exactly as I do, feel free to use the text as is (or use some of mine and supply your own for the rest.) The first and last items on my list, however, are essential to the play, and if you don't believe those, then I would ask that you not perform the play.*]

# Intradermal Nevus Envy

**HEATHER:**

The sun bunnies lounge in the beach chairs, lifting their glasses to search for their diet colas, and I look at them with envy.

Sunbathing, the ladies of the country club where I am working for the day, are sunbathing. Well, it's less expensive than golf. I don't look that closely, but I can surmise what they are reading, cheap summer paperback trash—I'd probably do the same in their position. They are sometimes reading but mostly trying to get tan. That is their goal, this summer, every summer, and I hate them for their ability to do just that.

Not just that I cannot suntan—$900 worth of doctor's bills for removal of suspicious looking moles means that I will never walk outside again without SPF 15 covering just about all of me, but where do these women find the time? To sunbathe?

It's because they don't work. Or that's what I'd like to think. Maybe they're all cocktail waitresses, maybe they all are cashiers at Jewel on the overnight shift, maybe they're all schoolteachers, but I doubt it, and it's easier to believe that this is what they spend their summer doing, baking their skin, and I wish skin cancer on each one of them, just out of jealousy, just to be spiteful, just because I'm running on nothing but negative energy these days, and it's a lot easier to have a few venomous thoughts than spend a half hour meditating each morning. And I think of friends who will tell me it's those venomous thoughts that landed me at the doctor's office, so I wish a little pain on them, too.

CURTAIN

# Nightmare run-on paragraph about a woman I forget.

[*Spotlight on Geryll on top of a ladder. She is lying on her stomach, feet straight out—like flying. The text is delivered at top speed.*]

**GERYLL:**
There was this girl, well really she was a woman she was grown and I was not altho I thought I was, but there she was and there I was and I liked her and she liked me and so we got in love and we made friends and we slept in the bed together and everything was not o.k.. It was not o.k.. Things were not o.k. between me and this lady that I try not to think or talk too much about they were not o.k. but I pretended that they were, even tho I cried, I cried everyday that I was giving, wasting, letting be sucked away—and then the fighting and then the fighting began and it was ugly and loud and long and people got hurt they got hurt in everyway everyway that is that people can get hurt and it was ugly and it was years not days anymore that were going by but this lady this lady and myself were at a loss—we had been captured in captivity colonized by each other and what was there to do—a rebellion a rebellion takes lots of people and lots of energy and there was only one of us, one of each desperate ones with no energy or joy or ecstasy and so we threw things we threw things like bowls and punches and threats and nasty little pieces of button pushing information that only the ones that you are most intimate with know about and we tried to kill each other to kill each other and I think we succeeded because there are parts of me little parts of me that I believe are dead, have died, beyond resuscitation and I'm sure she has those same parts that are different that mine but the same nonetheless in that they are dead. And I think of her, I think of her sometimes and I shudder at my ability to be so mean and ruthless and stupid and caring and violent and wrong and I put it away I put it away somewhere I rarely look somewhere nobody looks like in the back of my sock drawer or behind the toilet and I forget I forget quickly and fast and I don't like to talk about it I don't like to think about her, but right now I'm wondering, I don't want to but I'm wondering to myself where she is and what she's doing and how many pieces of her are dead because of me.

CURTAIN

# The Concussion Diet

[*Marjorie has a doll and a horsey with a saddle and demonstrates what happened. Performed in late night commercial style.*]

**MARJORIE:**

I've inadvertently stumbled upon a new way to lose weight and I want to share it with you. Fall off a horse and suffer a head injury. It worked for me and I'm sure it can work for you. Here's all you need to do. [*Places horse and rider on podium.*] Get on a horse. Don't tighten the cinch on the saddle quite enough. The horse will usually help you with this by puffing up as you attempt to secure the girth. Be sure to wear a helmet. You only want a concussion here—not a coma. Ride along casually. No need for fancy galloping, jumping or even trotting. As the saddle lists to one side and you're beginning to think you should dismount and tighten it, ignore that instinct for survival and allow the saddle to slowly slide around a la an episode of *I Love Lucy*. Hopefully, you too will strike your head with just the right force in just the right spot. Now I wish I could tell you where and how hard but I don't remember a damn thing that happened until I woke up, in the emergency room. But what could have turned into a horrible tragedy [*puts doll's hand to head in "woe is me" pose*] was actually a windfall. [*Raises doll's arms over head in triumph and makes it jump up and down.*] Miraculously, ever since the accident my appetite has been markedly diminished. At first, I thought it was just a temporary side effect but it's been nine months. I believe this method is as safe and effective as some of those other medical procedures and so-called weight loss systems that promise instant results without proper diet and exercise. And it's free! You don'thave to pay a dime. Just make sure you do it on someone else's property so their homeowners insurance will have to foot your medical bill. Oh sure, you'll have to have X-rays and a CAT scan and a stay in the hospital. You'll have to risk the possibility of short or long term memory loss, an atrophied cerebellum, loss of your motor skills or capacity for speech, life as a vegetable or even death; but so what? It's worth it! It's fast, it's free and it's as easy as falling off a... [*Marjorie zones out; if audience supplies proper word, says "horse." If not, calls:*]

CURTAIN

# Tiny Satan Play, Or How Evil Came To Vex a Friendly Pig

[*A campfire sing along and puppet show featuring a small, red, papier-mâché devil from Mexico, a medium-sized black ceramic pig and a rectangular green plastic basket large enough for the pig to sit in. The play takes place on top of a small table behind which Anita sits manipulating the objects. The column on the right indicates the puppet action.*]

**ANITA:**

When Satan was a tiny baby
Satan had no friends
His mother left him all day long
Stuck in his play pen!

*Satan alone on the table.*

*Anita slaps basket onto table and sticks Satan in it.*

*Chorus:*
Tiny Satan all alone
Tiny Satan baby
Tiny Satan all alone
Soon he will be hating.
Ba-dum bum bum!

*Satan peeks out the top of the basket.*

*Basket is removed.*

When Satan was a piddee lad
His little life was hard
His parents made him go and play
alone in the back yard.

*Satan walks forlornly across the table alone.*

Oh!
*Chorus*

Just as Satan went outside,
the rain came in a flood, whoosh!
Tiny Satan slip and slide
Fell down in the mud.

*Anita knocks Satan's feet out from under him, he lands face down.*

Tiny Satan is angry now
Dance a filthy jig
And in his rage and fury
His eye fell on a pig.

*Satan jumps up and dances angrily.*

*Pig, in the basket, is placed on the table; Satan sees Pig.*

Oh!
*Chorus*

The pig, it didn't bother none
Alone in its small pen
But Tiny Satan saw in it
His total lack of friends.

The pig, it gave a little smile                    *Pig is tilted out of basket to*
as if to say hello                                          *reveal smile.*
and that was the beginning
of a friendly pig's dire woe.

Oh! Tiny Satan all alone                          *Satan stalks Pig and begins*
Tiny Satan baby                                         *vexing Pig by shouting in*
Tiny Satan not alone                                          *Pig's ear.*
A pig he's now berating

Tiny Satan all alone                                *Satan flies above Pig's head.*
Tiny Satan baby
Tiny Satan don't know love                    *Satan held still high above*
So all he do is hating                                        *Pig's head.*
Ba-dum bum bum!                               *Satan drops onto Pig's head and*
                                                                           *dances.*

CURTAIN

# Witness

[*Phil speaks while two others are setting up a long table and two chairs.*]

**PHIL:**

The first time I did it I was drunk. It was after a concert. I remember a few years earlier I had seen *Jesus of Montreal*. Really good movie. Rent it if you get a chance. And then I was reminded of it from the news the other day. They're considering including them with your tax returns. I look at mine sometimes and I think, well, those people were right in a way. This is just a container. Not that that makes me want to end my life, but when my life does end why not let somebody else use it. Y'know, the parts they can anyway. My witnesses are Laura and Jim. Their names are still on there. If there's anyone here who hasn't signed the back of their driver's license to be an organ donor, perhaps you'd like to do it now? You can pick whichever two Neo-Futurists you'd like to be your witnesses.

[*This takes place.*]

Congratulations. You've saved a life today.

CURTAIN

# drag

*[Lusia sits in a chair facing the audience, backlit. She lights a cigarette, inhales, exhales. Exhales are magnified by other performers in different parts of the room exhaling when Lusia does. She addresses the audience.]*

## LUSIA:

*[Exhales.]* I smoke for the effect.

When I started I hid them in my neighbor's bushes.

My mother would smell me when I came home. *[Drags.]*

I denied everything. *[Exhales.]*

We sit in the smoking section now.

The first time I lit one in front of her directly correlates with the first time I told her I didn't believe in God.

It sounded something like this. *[She screams "I don't believe in God!" in Ukrainian. Exhales.]*

And I was throwing my clothes into a garbage bag.

She let me smoke so I would sit down. So I wouldn't leave.

I lit. *[Drags.]* I stayed. *[Exhales.]*

When I listen to my voice on tape I don't understand why people like it.

I got through college doing phone sex. *[Drags.]*

I could do my dishes while I worked. *[Exhales.]*

First pack purchase: 12 years old—85 cents.

I'm 30 now. I've paid three-fifty.

They're under $2.00 in Atlanta.

I have not gone out with men because they did not smoke.

Vice versa cubed, I assume.

I have walked more than a mile at 2 a.m. in January to avoid waking up without them. *[Drags.]*

Really. *[Exhales.]*

I have smoked other peoples' cigarette butts.

I felt a need to specify the nature of "butts" there.

Wouldn't want you to get the wrong impression. [*Drags. Exhales.*]

That would be a different play. [*Exhales.*]

I know a guy who liked to have the bottoms of his feet burned with a cigarette. [*Drags and strikes a pose in profile.*]

Glamour. [*Exhales.*]

My father died of cancer. My mother survived it. [*Stops with cigarette almost to lips.*]

Not lung cancer, though.

Last week, when discussing my unorganized tax situation I asked with wide eyed sincerity, "Do you think the IRS would try *me* as an adult?"

Funny how the mind works. [*Drags. Exhales.*]

Studies say I'm killing you right now.

Sorry.

[*As lights fade to black:*]

God, I'm scared I can't stop.

It's the effect.

CURTAIN

# Missing

[*There is a side light shining on the right side of one empty chair that is sitting a few feet right of center. It casts a long shadow of the empty chair across the stage. Noelle stands center behind the shadow in the darkness.*]

**NOELLE:**

I'm looking for someone. I wonder if you've seen her, but my guess is that you haven't. Not lately. She's been missing for years, I think, but I just noticed. I'll know her instantly if I see her again, though. She is bold and outspoken. She goes out of her way to befriend the friendless— defend the helpless. She's the kind of person who carries her homemade petition from door to door, neighborhood to neighborhood, until her blisters bleed, to save the world from tyranny and injustice.

I miss her when the homeless man on the corner asks me for change, and I shake my head and walk quickly by. I need her...when the mentally handicapped woman behind the counter is slow to make change, and I feel myself becoming annoyed.

I'm looking for someone who, as a child, spent much of her time looking forward to the grand person she knew she would someday be. But I find myself looking in the mirror at an adult who spends too little of her time looking back at the grand person she once was.

CURTAIN

# How I Forget to Remember You

[*Rob delivers text while walking quickly around and around a round table and a chair. On the table are a sheet of paper and a pen.*]

**ROB:**
I just have to
I just have to sit
I just have to sit down and write to write.
Otherwise I don't.
I don't.

I just have to
I just have to forget
I just have to forget it all to write.

I have to forget

        the dishes
        the laundry
        the bills
        the shopping
        the clog in the tub
        and the roaches in the cupboard

    forget

        the trucks and sirens
        the hissing from the heater
        the singing from below me
        and the shouting from above

    and the television
I have to forget the television and the vcr.

I just have to
I just have to forget it
I just have to really forget it to write.

I do.
And you.
You.

I just have to
I just have to forget you
I just have to forget you to write about you.

I do too.
And that's why I haven't called or stopped by
        or why we haven't gotten together

                                        for a coffee
                                        or a movie
                                        or a drink.

        'Cause I've written
                I have written
                I have
                Oh, not to you, but about you, I have written.

I have forgotten it all and written.

Not about your cheeks
        or eyes or lips
        or breasts or feet
        or hair or anything like that,
        that has been done.
I would not say you're nothing like the sun.

I would just ask that you understand the tasks before me
        what is daily at hand too often distracts me
        takes focus and keeps me away from this . . .

                                        this . . .
                                        this.

[*Rob sits at table.*]

But today, like I have for several before
I have just
I have just sat down
I have just sat down to write something.
I have just gotten up and sat down and forgotten it all to write

                        anything.

But I want you to see
            to see
            that you are written in and included, believe me
            when I say 'you are written in and included'
            when I sit down and forget
            to write.

[*Rob tries to write a bit.*]

CURTAIN

# This Is Not a Flattering Story

[*Heather is sitting in a harsh front spot, upstage right.*]

**HEATHER:**

It's 3:15 on a Monday afternoon. I've just had my fifth cup of coffee, and I'm almost, but not quite, running late. A woman in a new Lexus pulls up next to me; I give her the yes-I'm-leaving-this-spot nod, put my car into reverse, and notice that she is double-parking her car, getting out and walking her daughter into the Gus Giordano dance center. I honk my horn. I honk again, I am stunned by this woman's impoliteness. She is actually double-parking her car and walking inside. It's as if I do not exist.

I consider hitting her car with mine. I finger my keys, silently deciding which one is going to leave the biggest scrape of the side of her car. I pray for a tow truck.

Six and a half minutes elapse.

Visibly shaking with anger, I walk into the Gus Giordano dance center, where, at the top of the stairs, I see the woman amiably chatting with a group of mothers, and I snap. Every time I've been wronged and victimized in my 32 years—did I mention it was my birthday?—floods back into my mind, and I instantly think of the most horrible thing I could do to this woman.

I will walk over to her daughter, and very calmly, and quietly and menacingly tell her that her mommy has done something very wrong, and now something very bad will happen to her mommy, and she will never see her mommy again.

And as I walk down the stairway, out the door, down the block, who gives a fuck about the car at this point, I will hear that small child screaming and screaming, psychologically scarred for who knows how long.

I don't, of course. I simply tell the woman she needs to move her car — now—and then I walk downstairs. But I can see I've scared the group of them. It'll be a long time before any of them parks illegally again. And I hope I will be able to keep my anger in check.

CURTAIN

# Dame Fortuna's
# Popsicle Stick of Chance

**DAVID:**

As a boy I was fascinated by disaster. My G.I. Joe was forever crawling out from under landslides or pulling my sisters' Barbies from the wreckage of her tornado-torn dream pad. Any action figures I had were in constant peril of being blown to smithereens in their lean-to houses made of sticks by a cinder block meteorite.

What intrigued me most about these scenarios in my mind as well as on the news or in the daily papers was not the death tolls—who and how many died—but rather who and how many survived. Who lived to tell the tale? Did the person who switched airplane seats at the last second survive the crash only to find the person he had switched with had died?

[*David draws a small circle in chalk on the floor as he speaks.*]

As a boy, I would sometimes draw circles of chalk on the sidewalk behind my parents' house. I'd draw these circles—not very large—and I'd arm myself with a popsicle stick—and any ant—any little brown ant doing his anty best bringing food or news to the nest—any ant that strayed—by CHANCE into my chalk circle—got it.

Click.

Click.

Click.

Their tiny little exoskeletons cracking beneath my Popsicle stick.

Click.

[*Draws a large circle in chalk around himself and the small circle as he speaks.*]

At 33 I'm still fascinated by disaster. Guiltily I watch news of earthquakes, tornadoes, hurricanes and airline crashes—hoping to catch some survivor's tale of what it was like to have survived. At 33 I am often amazed that I am still here. In a fairly dangerous city. One where I ride my bicycle through busy city streets. And I've taken a lot of chances on the long road to getting here. Driving West Virginia mountain switchbacks during a blizzard. Walking, late at night, alone through New York's

Alphabet City a little bit drunk—a lot high. Climbing in rocky ravines ignoring the Keep Out Danger signs. Engaging in questionably safe sex with a man I'd met only twenty minutes before. Walking across a frozen quarry lake—the ice creaking beneath my feet.

At 33 I'm very aware of the chalk circle of my fragile G.I. Joe tiny little ant existence. And every day I wake up—take a deep breath and hope to stay one step ahead of the Popsicle stick of chance.

CURTAIN

# Born at the Tender Age of 18,
# He Died as an Infant,
# Nestled Safely in his Mother's Womb

**SCOTT:**

He was born with a mighty wallop of rubber on concrete, as the great green Impala picked up the pieces of his skull and suddenly reassembled it on his neck. To his friends in the car, he looked like a bag of garbage, as they receded in the distance, growing more and more drunk, until they would meet up at the bar where friendly men would pay them a dollar a pop for the beer they had inside them, where they would use pool cues to coax the balls from the pockets until all 15 were aligned in a perfect triangle in the middle of the soft green table. They would suck sweet marijuana smoke out of the air, pushing it into tightly wound joints, forcing butane back into lighters, unwrapping the papers and stuffing the sticky green buds into smooth plastic baggies. He would go to high school, where he would surrender his diploma and remove his cap and gown for the privilege of forgetting everything he ever knew. But instead of forgetting, he spent most of his time erasing pictures: fantastic drawings of demons, super heroes and other things not of this world. He would spend hours peeling paint off of hard statues, that he would later convert into soft green clay and mold into neat square blocks. Soon, he would stop getting high, stop drinking and stop smoking. He would spend more time inside class instead of outside breathing smoke into cigarettes that he and his friends would sell to vending machines and obliging clerks, whose profits he would carefully place in his mother's purse when she wasn't looking. He now had higher expectations for himself, giving his teachers report cards full A's & B's instead of C's, D's & F's. He laughed more and slept less. His eyes were no longer blood shot. He stopped going to school one day which made him very sad, for he cried and cried until his mother picked him up and then he was happy again. And even though he was smaller and had forgotten a great many things, he and his mother now got along fine now. No more suspicions. No more arguments. Until one day, after he had filled his mother's breasts with milk for one last time, he climbed into her womb, where nestled tightly and safely against the dangers of the world, he finally died.

CURTAIN

# I'm a Secretary!

© 1994 Dave Awl

[*Dave sits on a rotating stool center stage, with his back to the audience. He delivers the first "Yes, oh yes" facing upstage, then twists halfway and delivers the words "what you've heard about me is true" over his shoulder to the audience. He rotates to face the audience directly before saying the words "I'm a secretary." This is all done in an exaggerated tone of confessional melodrama. The rest of the monologue is performed in a dishy, effervescent manner which on one occasion led a prominent Chicago reviewer to refer to Dave as a "fey clown."*]

**DAVE:**

Yes, oh yes, what you've heard about me is true: I'm a secretary.

I'm not sure when this first dawned on me, the precise realization of it. I mean, the temporary agencies I work for used phrases like "word processor" and "office worker" and even when I first started working I was thinking things like "receptionist" or "typist" or "assistant to the big head of romaine lettuce in the corner office."

And then one morning at the "beverage station" someone casually referred to me as "Mike Dugan's secretary" and the whole fascinating realization of it came crashing down on me like a loose chunk of ceiling during a mild tropical earthquake. A secretary! How unspeakably quaint and disturbing! Suddenly I'm thinking *Thoroughly Modern Millie*, I'm thinking Mary Ann Singleton, I'm thinking Mr. Tudball and Mrs. A-Wiggins. Miss Fleen, can you come in here and take a letter—*please!* These were never my role models as a boy!

Oh, I don't mean to imply that I never had feminine role models growing up, but it was always, say, Marie Curie or Madame Blavatsky. You know, things like scientist, poet or chanteuse. "Secretary" just sounded so dowdy, so matronly, so...D-cup.

And then I realize I'm not just a secretary, I'm a *male secretary*. The first time I remember ever hearing these words was in the course of a homophobic letter to Ann Landers I read as a child. [*Moron voice*] "Dear Ann: Last week my husband ran away with his secretary. His *male* secretary! What's a girl to *do?*" And suddenly I'm not sure if my pants are tight enough to be a *male secretary*, oh he's pretty but can he type? [*He jumps as if pinched from behind*]—*Mr. Johnson!* I'll thank you to keep your eyes in your head as I am a highly skilled professional and I am not here for your *titillation!*

Oh, the baggage, the stereotypes, the misconceptions that my sisters in shorthand and I have to put up with. I realize that I have made my way into what has got to be one of the most misunderstood and under-estimated professions going, along with flight attendant, folk singer, and [*air quotes*] "fluffer."

You know, when I first started this my images of secretarial work were straight out of Dagwood and Blondie. But in reality, I saw dignified women and men in positions of skill and trust, and I began to realize that the people in the wall and corner offices were actually subservient in a way to their secretaries, helpless without them, like overgrown children—unable to operate the space-age equipment surrounding them or organize their simplest thoughts without the help of my esteemed colleagues.

And so I have come to respect and revere my secretarial co-workers. [*Merrily*] And sometimes, when all of us are lounging around the secretarial pool sipping margaritas, talking about tab stops and carriage returns, I weep for the untold millions, the "common people" who will never know what all those extra buttons on the phone are really for. How tragic, I think, how...*unlived.*

CURTAIN

# Victorious Secret

*[Lusia, with her back to the audience, reveals a large, dusty mirror. The mirror stands against the upstage wall and faces the audience. (Note: Baby powder is good for dusting down the mirror but be careful as it can make a stage floor very slippery.) Throughout the monologue she cleans the mirror with glass cleaner and a rag so the audience can see her by the end.]*

**LUSIA:**

I have come to believe, that if necessary, I could legitimately join the ranks of the insane.

You see, I found that a Victoria's Secret catalogue, with a little help from me, I must admit, can really fuck me up. This was verified last week. I came home last Thursday. I was tired. I walked downstairs and on the coffee table was a Victoria's Secret catalogue.

I was tired. I walked over to the couch—sat down—slumped down, really—so that my thighs spread out and the roll on my stomach could make itself uncomfortably apparent—and I picked the magazine up. I'm a determined young lady when it comes to this sort of thing. I opened it up and felt it start. Page after glossy page, I stared at these women in all their airbrushed splendor and with all the self-centeredness I could muster, I began hating not them but myself. I compared myself—my large Slavic self—to each of the willowy creatures sprawled out in front of me. Not consciously, you know, but...well...envy is nothing new for me. It's one of the Seven Deadlies I'm really good at. And self-degradation has proved to be a luxury of convenience and comfort. I put the magazine down, walked into my room, took my clothes off and stood in my lingerie (a pair of white cotton Jockey for Hers and a jog bra) in front of a four by six foot mirror under bright basement lights. I stood there a moment, just long enough to feel...oh...despair. And then I made a rational, centered, affirming decision. Within thirty seconds, I was in the kitchen at the fridge, the third cream cheese covered strawberry in my mouth.

Let the binge begin.

But then, miracle of miracles, something happened. I stopped for just a second and I really looked and really saw that, yes, indeed this was fairly, if not very, insane. Crazy.

Really. There's no reason to it. No sense in it. There was absolutely no rational thought present anywhere in this cycle. I've been told that there is freedom in reality. Reality, my reality, is that I, with a little help from a Victoria's Secret catalogue have the capacity to really, really fuck myself up. Whatever the reason for these spiritual suicides may be is inconsequential, because right now, the primary thing I care about, I'm grateful to say, is that that night the Victoria's Secret went into the garbage. Not me.

CURTAIN

# Reconnaissance

*[The text below is either pre-recorded or delivered live by Connor. Connor is on stage with all necessary props in a small box or suitcase. Already set are a table and two chairs. As the text is heard, the following will happen:*

*Connor puts a pair of dress shoes on the floor in front of one of the chairs.*

*Connor drapes dress pants over the seat of and down the legs of this chair, securing the garment with clothespins or rope.*

*Connor hangs a rope so that it is suspended above the chair and hangs a dress shirt, tie and suit jacket from this rope so that it hangs in front of the back of the chair. (Note: another solution to this is to set a ladder behind the chair and hang the shirt, tie and jacket from one of the rungs on this ladder).*

*Connor attaches a hat to the rope using a clothespin (or puts it atop the ladder).*

*Connor displays a sign that reads "DAD" and attaches it to the suit jacket with a clothespin.*

*Connor sets the table with a teapot, a cup and a saucer.*

*Connor sits and pours himself tea. He sips and waits a moment then nervously sets his tea down and pours tea for "DAD." With the absence of an additional cup, however, the tea spills onto the table and dribbles onto the floor.]*

## CONNOR:

Let us consider the native cultures of the Pacific Islands. During World War II, the Pacific Islands were overrun with Allied troops and equipment. The natives, having no previous contact with the West, suddenly found themselves surrounded by enormous wealth and technology. Throughout the war, this wealth and technology trickled down to these people through the black market. After a time, the natives became aware that they were only receiving left-over and hand-me-down equipment from the soldiers. Furthermore, the natives believed that this wealth and equipment were gifts from the gods. Gifts that were unfairly passing through the hands of the soldiers first. Not content with this slow trickle of wealth, and especially disappointed when the soldiers left and the trickle stopped altogether, some of the natives sought to explain why the gods had stopped sending gifts. Moreover, these people wanted to correct the problem and have the wealth return. Thus, the Cargo Cults were born.

For all of these cults, the sky was a key concept. The gods, they believed, lived in the sky and would send huge, silver birds to deliver their gifts. According to the cults, all the soldiers did was provide these birds with a place to drop off the gifts. They did this by building airstrips and control towers. So it followed that the Cargo Cults had only to build their own airstrips—their own control towers—and then these silver birds would visit them. So that is what the Cargo Cults did. Throughout the Pacific Islands, they arranged things to look like airstrips, clearing acres of forest, lighting fires that would line the edges of this cleared land.

They would build tall wooden towers next to the cleared land and would take turns sitting inside the towers. They would take turns being the controller and would wear pieces of wood on their heads that were carved to look like headphones. They would mount bamboo poles on to the towers and on to wooden boxes painted to look like radios. They would go to great lengths to make sure the airstrip was level and that the tower was high enough and that the radio knobs were painted well. And then they would wait, they would wait for the silver birds to land.

CURTAIN

# Not Even a Neo-Futurist Can Live on Bread Alone

*[Phil is stage right in a spotlight with a Hostess Cherry Pie™.]*

**PHIL:**

I love Hostess Cherry Pies. I've loved them as long as I can remember. The doughy crust with that little white powdered stuff on the outside. The filling.

I know that I can count on Hostess Cherry Pies to be there when I want one. No matter where I get one I know they'll always taste the same and look the same and I love that.

I could spend the rest of my life eating no snack cake other than Hostess Cherry Pies and be a very happy man.

I just wanted to take this opportunity to announce my love for Hostess Cherry Pies in front of all of you and my friends here in the show and in front of god. I love Hostess Cherry Pies.

*[Lights up stage left on Stephanie lighting the candle on a beautiful birthday cake. Phil turns to look at it. Turns back to audience. Pause.]*

Do you think it'd be alright if I just put my finger in it?

CURTAIN

# Bead Goddess

©1999 Marjorie Fitzsimmons

**MARJORIE:**

Mardi Gras, New Orleans—The Big Easy. Debauchery, parades, hundreds of thousands of people from all over the world carousing in the Quarter, the wail of blues, beignets and coffee at 3 a.m. at Café Du Monde, Lafitte's, crawfish étouffée, laissez les bon temps rouler, Geneviève Bujold, Au Revoir Les Enfant, Maurice Chevalier. Those last few don't have anything to do with it, I just like to say things with a French accent. There is one Mardi Gras tradition that I revel in more than any other. Working it for these. [*Displays big beads.*] The beads. These cheap plastic bits of crap. You know how you get them? [*Waits for answer from audience, responds accordingly.*] You flash your tits and people throw them to you from the balconies. That's the way you get the good ones anyway. What possesses me to engage in this exploitive, puerile beading frenzy? Status. Normally, I could give a shit but in this specific time, in this particular place, I crave it. You're probably thinking I'm an exhibitionist and you're right but it goes beyond that. It becomes ritual. When I sashay down Rue Bourbon swathed in beads up to my ears and down to my ankles people stop sucking down their hurricanes and daiquiris and nitrous oxide filled balloons and smile and stare in wonder. I have more, bigger, better, brighter, longer, fatter and shinier beads than anybody. Every few hours I have to go back to the car to de-bead because my neck starts to ache from the weight. A man on a balcony spots me in the throng and beckons—dangling the beads like a hypnotist's watch. In a practiced, yet alluring manner, I slowly raise my shirt revealing my universally proclaimed perky breasts. Cheers, catcalls, methodic nods of approval and then: the throw. The shimmering beads hurtle through the air my hand stretches and scoops them out of free fall. Ceremoniously, I adorn myself. I relish my notoriety—fleeting and anonymous. As I move on to my next score, above the celebratory din, a stranger calls out, "Hey, bead goddess." I know he's talking to me.

CURTAIN

# To the Noodle

© 1997 David Kodeski

[*David speaks mostly to Steph's pregnant belly.*]

**DAVID:**

My mother—from her late twenties to mid-thirties—good Catholic that she was—spent the better part of her days in a state of perpetual pregnancy. I'm the second oldest of seven—so I changed lots of shitty diapers and cleaned up lots and lots of spittle and goo. I don't hold it against any of you...and it's nothing personal—but I really don't like babies too much...I'm not good at small talk with them... [*longish silence*] ...Well! Because my mom was pregnant a lot, I also got to feel a lot of my brothers and sisters squishing around in my mother's guts before they were born. When there were more of us out here than there were to come—we'd sometimes fight over who got to feel ma's belly.

[*General confusion as "It's my turn! I didn't get a turn! You just had a turn!", etc., is shouted from the sides.*]

We'd watch *The 21st Century* with Walter Cronkite on Sunday nights—pressing against mom's belly and the brother or sister that was inside.

I should tell you—some of my siblings are on Prozac now. Not because of the pressing—but because of the PRESSING... the world around us... go go go! Work work work!

Also, your mom? One of these days you're going to say something really really mean and shitty at her...for how stupid she is—or how she just doesn't get it—or just 'Cause she's a fucking drag, man...you may not believe that now...but you will. We all do.

There's a lot of meanness out here. But today, I saw a robin. And there's this comet in the sky that your mom and dad will sure tell you about—the one that was up there—when you were...in here...

I guess, all I want to say is, you know, good luck and all of that. And—um—[*silence*]—well, let's talk about this in 2015...that's all I guess.

CURTAIN

# Our Story Thus Far

[*Ayun sits on stage, shaving her hairy legs, while the following text is heard in a taped voice over.*]

**AYUN:**

I moved to New York City in the summer of metallic shirts and platform shoes. It was not 1974, but you couldn't tell by the clothes. I rode a bicycle and was told I would be killed for doing so. Every day the doorman would tell me about the weather and then I would pedal away on my bicycle. So far I am still alive. I began to carry a backpack for the times when I harvested the fruits and vegetables that grew on the sidewalks beneath green and white awnings. I don't really know if the awnings are green and white... I have already started to change them for my memory of the summer I moved to New York, the summer of metallic shirts and platform shoes and my wedding dress hanging in the closet. Sometimes someone would ask me if I missed Chicago. Whenever anyone asked me if I missed Chicago, if I miss Chicago, I felt like flinging my arms around that person's neck. I feel my heart kicking its heavy booted foot against the walls of my chest. My heart wears the same kind of boots as Karen, the friend who is home in Chicago, who I miss every day. Also Lisa and the bucket of compost on my back porch in which I could watch the world decompose for hours on end. When this happens, I have to shop for fruit. I have to get on my bicycle and ride. I lived in Chicago for eleven years and I never once shaved my legs. It'll grow back.

CURTAIN

# Natural Born Woman

[*Ayun stands holding a boom box which plays Cowboy Junkies' version of "Sweet Jane." Sways dreamily to the music, voice is passive, feminine, with a calculated lack of guile, eyes focus on the middle distance, a little strangely.*]

**AYUN:**

Y'know what, Mickey? Sometimes...sometimes I wish I was a little vixen in a movie and I'd be played by Juliette Lewis or Patricia Arquette and my name'd be Alabama or Memphis or Turquoise. I'd be real stupid, but I was abused when I was little so I'm sweet and kind of childlike and real tragic and everything.

[*Pause.*]

And what some would call good fuckin' I call true love. I'd say, "Y'know what, Mickey? When they come to get us,"—'coz sooner or later somebody's gonna have to come get us since we shot a lot of innocent people, well, mostly just waitresses and truckers and my mom and dad— "When they come to get us, I'm gonna turn into a big red horse, carry you on my back all the way up to the stars!"

I won't remember when Daisy Buchanan told Jay Gatsby she was gonna push him around in a big pink cloud. That's not one of my reference points. I'm not allowed to read. I watch TV... even though I know it's not very good for me. If I was more self-reflexive I'd think that line about the red horse was real original.

Look at me dance.

CURTAIN

# leaving/falling

[*Chloë is sitting at a table, in a spotlight, a glass bowl in front of her filled with sand. She scoops some sand out of a bowl and lets it run through her fingers.*]

**CHLOË:**

I have taken a pin and engraved your name on each grain of this sand.

[*Lights fade out as the sand runs through her fingers.*]

CURTAIN

# Joke

[*Blackout. A door to the street opens abruptly to reveal Greg standing in the threshold facing the audience. The only light comes from the street. Bill can be seen lying on the sidewalk just beyond the door. As Greg delivers the following text, Bill raises himself onto his elbows and asks passers-by if they'll remember him when he's gone.*]

**GREG:**

A man wearing pajamas walks into a bar and says "How can we understand the idea of pain when we don't feel pain? How can we understand misery—other people's misery—when we don't feel misery ourselves?" The people in the bar swivel in their chairs and their stools to better hear the man, they carry their drinks as they turn. "I passed a woman on the sidewalk the other day," says the man, "she was lying on her side. Asleep. A dark line on the pavement traced a trail of urine from her pants to the gutter, her skin was burnt and hard from living under the sun, and wrinkles formed like welts under her eyes. I woke the woman up to ask if she was alright and she said, 'No. I'm not all right.' And it didn't seem to matter to me. I walked on and she fell back to sleep. The next day I returned to the same spot only to discover a crowd mingling around the body of the woman, and an ambulance parked at the gutter to take her remains away. When they picked her body up to put it on the gurney her head dangled below her neck for a moment and her hair swept the pavement like broom. A man beside me murmured 'good riddance to bad garbage,' and I couldn't bring myself to disagree with him. I walked home and went to sleep. I awoke that night with the clearest premonition of my own death and the deepest fear that most of the world would almost certainly not care. I feel the fear. But I don't miss the woman. I feel the fear so clearly, and I won't go home until it goes away. So I ask you, how can we can we understand the idea of pain—other people's pain—when we don't feel pain ourselves?" The bartender pours the man a drink and says, "We can't. So you better make yourself comfortable." And the man says, "That's what I want more than anything."

[*Bill continues questioning passers-by. The door slams shut.*]

CURTAIN

# Small Town 3

[*Ayun sits on the edge of the stage.*]

**AYUN:**

The only thing John ever did to distinguish himself was to die of AIDS. Previous to that, he was about as bad of an athlete as I was and a horrible student and a good artist in a neighborhood where all the children who were bad athletes were good artists and we always made him play the smallest part when we put on plays in Katie Ayers' garage. We made him play Auntie Em. He couldn't remember more than two lines at a time and even though I played at his house on a hundred or more occasions, I can't remember a single game that we played, just one time when Katie Ayers beat the shit out of him in the vacant lot, stuffed him full of snow, and his mother came out and yelled at both of us for picking on somebody weaker than ourselves even though John was 2 years older and she couldn't help herself, she yelled at John for letting himself get beat up by two little girls. Poor dumb John with his lisp and his freckles and that constant expression of buck-toothed good humor that made you want to pack his pants full of snow. Once at the lake, I heard his mother tell the other mothers, drunk and happy and laughing now that the children had been packed off to bed, that Michael, John's perfect older brother with his lawnmower and good manners was born perfect, and John, they got at a discount. He came in a do-it-yourself kit that they put together wrong, oh, ha ha ha ha ha ha ha ha, but this was all long ago, before my mother left my father to marry the man who lived two houses away, and the wife he left behind married the man in the house in between as soon as *his* wife died of cancer and my stepbrother suddenly found himself related to every kid in the neighborhood except Katie Ayers and perfect lawn-mowing Michael, and John, poor dumb buck-toothed John who had a red dog named Cinnamon and never did anything special unless you count dying of AIDS.

CURTAIN

# Vertigo

**DIANA:**

It's not heights I fear. No, it isn't heights. I can stand on the edge—have stood, in fact, on the edge of steep escarpments, dangerously close to the edge and looked down. I do not fear this. I fear hitting my head on things. Things like the ground. A cement curb. The pointed corner of the kitchen counter. The edge of the sink, the edge of the tub, the edge of really anything that has a good sharp one. Large, rough, craggy, granite rocks.

I look up vertigo in the dictionary. It is defined there as a subjective sensation of dizziness. As opposed to what? An objective sensation of dizziness? Are not all sensations, well, for want of a more accurate term, subjective? Isn't dizziness, by definition, subjective? I mean, it is not we who are whirling about uncontrollably, it is you who are having the sensation that things are akilter and spinning.

I associate vertigo—and I am not alone in this, I mean I'm not a pioneer here—with a fear of falling and with an almost irresistible desire to fall. I have been caught up short on precipitous and unstable mountainsides through the sheer force of my will and through my own undaunted stupidity. Twice, I have stood on the side of a mountain, an obtuse angle formed by the plane upon which I stand and the plane of my body, and I have experienced a sensation (purely subjective, I freely admit) that I call vertigo, but which is not dizziness at all. It is a moment, usually fleeting, in which the options become crystalline clear: You can fall here, too easily—misstep on this moist, black talus slope and you will go tumbling across the rock, bouncing off the sides of the cliff to land, nicked and bruised, bloody, battered and most certainly dead in an untidy clump on the wet grass, far below.

Or, girlfriend, you can jump. Before your head makes smacking impact with that particularly jagged-looking outcropping of rock which for some reason you can see so distinctly now below you that you might even want to aim for it, you will know the freedom of flight and the exhilaration of self-determination. It will be glorious, to see the rich, dark, shining shale in such detail, and to find the earth rushing up to meet you, like the kiss of a baby. It is as tempting and as real a physical desire as that, as to press lips against flesh. You can feel, standing there, how gratifying it will be to push off and sail.

It is not an internal debate, there is no weighing here of the pros and cons. There is only this enormous lucidity, this revelation of the two alternatives. And the—oh!—the desire to indulge in sensation.

The result, of course, is the same. You land, nicked and bruised, bloody, battered, etc. But the means, the means, there lies the difference.

There is a third option: you can turn your eyes upward and get the fuck off this fucking incline and up to the fucking ridge before you do something stupid.

The third option is generally the most popular, and though I usually prefer the road less traveled, I bow to convention on this point.

CURTAIN

# Talking To Myself

[*This monologue can be—and has been, many times—performed as a solo monologue with no special staging or tech. The more elaborate, optional staging described here requires several assistants, but can be adapted as needed for other circumstances. The piece begins in blackout. A pair of flashlights held by assistants click on to reveal Dave standing on stage, flanked by two large mirrors, held by two more assistants. For most of the piece, Dave speaks quickly and frenetically, except where noted.*]

**DAVE:**

So I'm talking to myself, talking to myself and I say [*to reflection on left*]: "Hi. What's your name?" [*To audience*] And myself says, "If you don't know, I'm not gonna tell you." And I say [*to reflection on right*], "Hey—why can't I ever get a straight answer?" [*To audience*] And myself says, "Look. I wear the same clothes as you, I eat the same food, I brush the same set of teeth. When you look in the mirror, it's my eyes you see." [*On the words "my eyes" he turns head to make eye contact with reflection, then looks forward again. Next line is directed forward.*] And I say, "I know all that. What I want to know is: who—the fuck—*are* you?"

[*Lights click off. Lights click back on to reveal Dave looking down into a large mirror held under his chin, but tilted so audience can see reflection. Second mirror is held behind his head.*]

My personal favorite episode of *Gilligan's Island* was the one where there was this giant spider that kept terrorizing everybody and taking the castaways hostage by trapping them in a little cave. The castaways tried to defeat the spider by rigging up a huge mirror on a bicycle, and then backing the spider into a corner by scaring it with its own reflection. And it was working until Gilligan broke the mirror (go, Gilligan.) Anyway, I was thinking about this a while back and I realized that what this is, is a kind of modern answer to the Greek myth of Narcissus. And what it says is that instead of being attracted by our own image, many of us in this day and age are incredibly repulsed. And this is very true. I know that if anyone ever wanted to back me into a corner, all they'd have to do is show me an image of myself and I'd run till I hit the wall.

[*Lights click off. They click back on to reveal Dave flanked by mirrors again.*]

And then some wise guy in the mirror says, "You know why that is, don't you? You're not talking about yourself, you're talking about the way you see yourself. They're two different things. Why, if the Way You See Yourself were to call Yourself up on the phone and ask it out on a date, Yourself would hang up."

And I say good point, I think.

[*Lights click off. When they click back on, Dave is seated with his back to audience, looking out at them from the mirrors which are held in front of him.*]

So I'm talking to myself, talking to myself, and I say: "Look, I don't understand. I never even knew you existed until I was almost grown up. And now you won't even talk to me." And myself says, "That's because you're afraid of me." And I say, "Look, I'm not afraid of myself. I'm afraid of what I am when I'm not myself!" And myself says [*a weary tone*]: "Then why do you always break your promises?"

[*Lights click off. They click back on to reveal Dave lying on his side with his head propped up on his elbow. One mirror is held at an angle behind him, the other lies on the floor in front of him. There is a change of mood here: Dave's tone of voice for the next section is suddenly quieter, calmer, more reflective. As if telling a ghost story around a campfire.*]

Look. Here's how it is. Once, a really long time ago, I was lying in bed trying to get to sleep, and I heard this loud knocking on the door. So I got up to go answer it, and when I opened the door there was no one there—I couldn't see a thing. So I go to get back in bed and when I get there, what do I see but myself, lying there in bed, just like I hadn't moved at all. So I say, hey, move over, I've really gotta get back in bed. And the other me looks up and says [*a quiet, even tone*], "Oh, no. You'll spend the rest of your life trying to get back in bed with me, and it'll never happen until you figure out why you left."

[*Lights off, then back on to reveal Dave sitting cross-legged on floor, flanked by mirrors. Back to original tone.*]

So I'm talking to myself, talking to myself, and I say: "Look, this is ridiculous. I feel like we've gotten very far away from our original subject." And myself says, "I know. That's my point."

[*Lights click off.*]

CURTAIN

# Shit Story with Bad Pirate Accent

*[Bill stands center stage, with eyepatch over eye. Text is delivered in horrid pirate accent. The word ARRRGH! is meant to represent that sound, you know, that pirates make.]*

**BILL:**

Once me brother was lookin' through the classifieds, tryin' ta find a job...ARRRGH! An' he was hungry fer some cereal, and tryin' ta findin' some, he ran across some bran, and he couldn't remember if bran was the type o' thing that stopped ya up or ran ya out o' town so's ta speak.... ARRRGH! But, with lots of sugar and some banana, he pours a big ol' bowl, and he's doin' just fine. So's about a half an hours later, he finds a photo assistantship he's qualified fer and he calls the number there's in the ad. But, he gets a phone machine, so, at the beep he says,

" 'Allo. My name is Robbie and I'm callin' fer the photo assistant job, my number is 718 852 989....

But, then he feels something warm running down his leg.

"Oh my God," he says, "that's shit."

Then he remembers he's still on the phone machine to his possible future boss and what his possible future boss has heard is,

" 'Allo. My name is Robbie and I'm callin' fer the photo assistant job, my number is 718 852 989.........oh my God, that's shit."

So, he quickly finishes up, "9892, feel free to call me anytime." He hangs up and waddles off to the bathroom, wondering if the guy will ever call him. And you know what, he didn't. ARRRRRGH!

CURTAIN

# Love, I shoulda stayed drunk

© 1997 Robert Neill

*[Rob finds an envelope on stage opens it and takes out a piece of paper.]*

**ROB:**
During a wild binge of drink
I wrote you a letter of love.
It being that time of year.
It started off 'My dearest dove,'
But you, I know now, received it not.

Alas, I did not use postage enough,
the declaration being bigger, than my stamp
would willingly support.
Thus back it came to me.

Excited just to get a note,
I noticed not that it was mine.

I thought the hand familiar, but was overwhelmed
by such words of love, devotion
and poetic declaration; so exquisite; so pure; how things only
occasionally rhymed, signed simply, 'Your love';

I thought this lovely bit of honey rightly flew
from you to me in a large and special postal plane
from your fair hand so far away—
A fair exchange, I thought;
I thought,

I thought, truly it must be from you.
But later when I sobered up,
I found the envelope 'Postage due'.
I knew: We once one; were two. . .

Separate people never to touch, to hold, to share again—
Fuck! How pathetic. You never sent me a . . . piece a. . . a
Nothing!

*[Rob crumples up paper and throws into the audience.]*

CURTAIN

# TWO MINUTES OR LESS

© 1995 Greg Kotis

[*Throughout the play Greg sprints to deliver cards from back stage to an audience member. Each card contains a line for the audience member to read. Greg waits for the audience member to read each card before sprinting back stage for the next one. Ayun watches the clock throughout, after two minutes she calls curtain.*]

CARD #1: Throughout this play, Greg will hand you cards with lines on them. Read the lines in quotation marks out loud. Now, look at Greg and say, "I understand."

CARD #2: "Greg and I are performing a play now."

CARD #3: "We don't have much time to do it."

CARD #4: "It's important that we finish all the plays tonight. If this play goes on longer than two minutes, Ayun will call it short."

CARD #5: "Greg is twenty-nine years old."

CARD #6: "Greg is depending on me to read these lines clearly and loudly. He won't give me another card until I finish reading this one."

CARD #7: "Or this one."

CARD #8: "And so on."

CARD #9: "This play is about control."

CARD #10: "Greg is starting to go grey. This is something new for him."

CARD #11: "At the beginning of this play, Greg handed me a card telling me what to do. Here's what it said."

CARD #12: "Throughout this play, Greg will hand you cards with lines on them. Read the lines in quotation marks out loud. Now look at Greg and say, 'I understand.'"

CARD #13: "Thats when I looked up at Greg and said 'I understand.'"

CARD #14: "Greg is worried about time."

CARD #15: "At this point in the play, Greg stops running back and forth to catch his breath."

CURTAIN

# What Happened

**AYUN:**

Something happened to me last year at about this time. I mean, it didn't so much happen to me as it happened to someone else, but I made it so that it happened to me, if that makes any sense. What happened was, I took this thing that happened to someone else and I wrote about what had happened and a lot of people read about it but it turns out it wasn't really mine to write about. At all. And if I'd've thought about it for two seconds, I would have known that.

I should say that what happened was really bad, about the worst thing that could have happened to anyone, and the only thing that could have made it worse would be if one of the people who this happened to had gotten raped as well. It was the kind of thing that, if it happened to me, I think I'd kill myself, or I hope I'd kill myself and about once a day I pray to the great random universe not to let a thing like what happened to them happen to me and I hope it never happens to any of you either.

Well anyway, what happened was, soon after I wrote about this terrible thing, I began to get a bad feeling in the pit of my stomach, and this was made worse when a few people I know who know the people this terrible thing happened to told me, "Hey, you know that thing you wrote? Well, it made the people that that terrible thing happened to feel even worse than they are feeling already!"

Oh my god I'm an asshole.

And then I got a letter from the people that the bad thing happened to.

And for the last year, not a day goes by that I don't think that I'm a despicable, attention-grubbing asshole and also, please god, don't let a thing like what happened to them happen to me.

But wait, the story gets better, because just when I was most wretched, another terrible thing happened. Not to me. Not to the people the first terrible thing happened to, but to someone else, someone I knew... slightly. And this time, I did something that made the terrible situation better. To a degree. I mean, you can't bring back the dead, but I did do something that I hope someone would do for me if it was me lying there on the broiling hot asphalt. And I thought, well maybe my behavior during the second terrible thing will lead to absolution for the first terrible thing that happened, but then what happened was:

I started telling the story of the second terrible thing pretty frequently, but not the first terrible thing, because I was ashamed of the first terrible thing, whereas the second terrible thing reflected well on me as a person, while still containing the high stakes drama of the first. And then I started thinking, what if it WAS me there on the asphalt?

And I realized that if I want absolution, I shouldn't allow myself to tell the second terrible thing without owning up to the first terrible thing. And my role in the first terrible thing is something I'm ashamed of, and the people that the first terrible thing happened to, the people who honestly experienced it as a brutal, unexpected tragedy, have made it clear that they consider that story *their* story and they're the only ones who can tell it right. And that it's incumbent on me to acknowledge that.

And I realized it would make a great book. I could write an amazing book about this. If nothing else, I could get on my favorite radio program and people hearing my story at home would react the way I react when I hear an incredible story. The two terrible things taken together, are the most profound and interesting things that have ever happened to me, except that they happened to someone else. People whose lives are now gone or in ruins. While I'm merely stuck with a wonderful story I can never tell. And the ongoing belief that maybe one day a terrible thing will happen to me so I can see how it feels instead of just acting like an asshole. And feeling like an asshole. Even now. I'm sorry.

CURTAIN

# Hop on Pop Culture

[*Rachel reads from the book* How the Grinch Stole Christmas *by Dr. Seuss but abandons it as she goes off on a tangent.*]

**RACHEL:**
All the Whos down in Whoville liked Christmas a lot,
But the tycoons who run Universal did not.
"This *Grinch*," they all cried, "Is just way too boring!
Why, this Dr. Seuss book has got everyone snoring!
And these illustrations? How simple! How quaint!
It's charming, but mega-blockbuster it ain't!"

So high in their suite on the twelvty-eighth floor
They puzzled and puzzed til' their puzzlers were sore.
Then they shouted "Eureka!" and danced and made merry
And got on their cell phones to call up Jim Carrey.

Then they dialed up Ron Howard and plied him with hooch!
They assembled a cast and one cute little pooch!
They built a big set with boop-zoopers and zonkers!
They threw in a love interest with big dinkle-donkers!

And the last thing they did, those Hollywood boys?
Why, they got down to work making tie-ins and toys!
They churned out Grinch posters, Grinch candy, Grinch dolls,
Grinch thing-a-ma-jigs on the shelves in the malls!

"It's brilliant!" they cackled and sipped Perrier,
"Now we just wait until Thanksgiving day,
When Who-children in Whovilles all over the nation
Will demand to go see this big Grinchy sensation!
And then when they're through, why, they'll all cry boo-hoo—
Unless they go home with a Grinch toy or two!"

And sure enough, when it opened, well, some people say
Universal's accounts grew three sizes that day.
And kids are still flocking to all take a look
At what once was cartoon, and before that, a book.

So toot your tang-tooklers and bomp your whomp-whuckers,
Because Hollywood finally stole Christmas. [*Pause.*] Those fuckers.

CURTAIN

# My Babci was an Immigrant

*[David stands in front of a map of Poland, stage left.]*

**DAVID:**

She was born here. *[David runs to a map of the U.S., stage right.]* She died here. *[David runs to map, stage left.]* She was born here... *[Pointing to a somewhat specific area in southwestern Poland.]* somewhere around here. In 1905 she was born somewhere around here. In 1905 she was born Anna Debski somewhere around here. She was baptized in the Catholic faith. *[Runs to map, stage right.]* She was Anna Kubarski—and a mother of one—when she arrived here by steamer the first time. Her husband was named John and he sent her back—pregnant with their second child. *[Runs to map, stage left.]* Why she returned is a bit of a family mystery as is the exact name of the exact village she returned to. She and her husband John were somewhat close lipped about their history. *[Runs to map, stage right.]* When she returned here she was a mother of two. For some reason she again either returned here—carrying their two children in her arms and one in her belly—*[Runs to map, stage left.]* or was sent back. The facts are unclear. *[Walks slowly back to stage right.]* She sailed back for a final time in 1936—pregnant and sick as a dog, she'd say—and gave birth soon after to my mother. She never returned to Poland. They settled in Niagara Falls, New York which is about 500 miles from here. *[He puts up an arrow facing East which reads "Niagara Falls: 500 miles."]* He made Shredded Wheat. *[David holds up a box of Shredded Wheat.]* Shredded Wheat your grandparents may have eaten for breakfast. When she was much older and widowed and working as a cleaning lady she often said she never wanted to go back to Poland—ever—because she was afraid she would die and be buried there. She loved this country. Unconditionally. This is more than I can say for myself. She also loved her religion. This is most certainly more than I can say for myself.

When I moved to Chicago she said, "It's so far." *[David looks to map, stage left.]* I traveled the 500 miles between here and Niagara Falls seven times in the last six years—this last time just a couple of weeks ago to attend her funeral. She was eighty-nine. And she is buried where she wanted to be. On American soil. Next to John. In a Catholic cemetery.

CURTAIN

# Make/Believe/Story

**CONNOR:**

I don't know where to put things anymore. I come to this theater week after week and I say things about myself and by saying them to you, they seem to lose their proper place in my mind. And afterwards, I don't know how to fit the information back into my head. So, in the end, everything I say about myself when I am in this place seems like a total fiction. The fact that I even sound concerned about this strikes me as inauthentic and not quite me. Perhaps because this play is so self-referential it is somehow a more accurate picture of who I am...but I don't consider myself to be very self-referential either.

Sometimes, someone else will say something about me.

[*Someone in the cast says something about Connor.*]

And these sorts of things always seem more believable than the things I say about myself. Why is that, do you think? Wouldn't it be more helpful if I asked myself that question?

There are so many things I wish I could tell you about myself. So many things I wish you would believe. So many versions of myself I could leave you with, each more accurate than this version.

[*He brings out a bag full of gloves.*]

Here, I want to tell you a story. But I need one of you to pick the story. I need to know I didn't choose the story, that there's nothing special about it. That it will still be mine after I've told it. After you've heard it. After you believe it.

[*He chooses an audience member to reach into the bag and pull out one glove. He tells the story of that glove. When the story is finished, Connor puts the glove on and shakes the audience member's hand.*]

CURTAIN

# Excuse Number Six
# for an Inefficient City

[*Bill stands center stage.*]

**BILL:**

It's okay when the tub doesn't drain. Now, I can take a shower or a bath........or both.

CURTAIN

# Hey Walt why do some things always remind us of others

[*Rob stands on stage near a table and holding a brown paper bag. Rob originally performed this play with the actual Bambi Lamp. However a simple, small, plain-looking lamp, may be substituted or even no lamp at all.*]

**ROB:**
'You can call me Flower
if you want to, Bambi.'
Bam  bi.
Bam  bi lamp.

I have a Bambi Lamp.
I found it, and it's mine.
I have a Bambi Lamp that
I found on a Chicago City train platform
in the trash
and now it's mine.
Someone's discarded trash. Mine.

I discovered this piece of      this
Bambi. Fire.  Run, Bambi, Run.  Man!
Man . . . man, on the southbound Belmont El platform
I found
this loveable lost little lam . . . p
huddling in the trash.

It couldn't have been there for long
for nothing was on top of it.
Nothing was on top of the two pieces—
The Bambi Lamp                 [*Rob removes lamp from bag.*]
And the Bambi Lamp Shade.      [*Rob removes shade from bag.*]

The two pieces were both there;
The two pieces possibly still intact.

I almost did not pick them up, at first,
Something must be wrong I thought—
Frayed cord. Broken switch. Holy shade.
I thought.
But then I thought again.

But then I thought again.
Why not?
I have no things Bambi at home.
If it works, I have a new Bambi Lamp.
And if it doesn't, I discard it in a dumpster
not far from where I found it.
So I rescued this Bambi from the bin
of coffee cups, tossed Tribs, and forgotten Times
never to be recycled,
And headed homeward.

I walked proudly down Belmont
passed the regular Belmont fare
of flannel punks and Neon St. kids
of Chicago Tattoos and Dunkin' Donuts.
Bambi Lamp and Shade in hand.

Bambi Lamp and Shade in hand;
I walked up Halsted and home.

Once there,
I screwed in the bulb,        [*Rob removes a bulb from bag,*
plopped on the shade,        *and proceeds to do the actions as described.*]
plugged in the plug,
and switch . . .        [*Stage lights go out as Rob turns the lamp on.*]

The light . . .
The light of the once forgotten,
The light of the once thought functionless,
The light of the forest once again fell from
The scenic Bambi Shade on to
Bambi with Blue Butterfly on tail
fell once again on
The green grassy base
fell again upon
The abridged Bambi Book
opened permanently to the
Birth of Bambi page

'What you gonna call the young Prince?,'
the little rabbit asked.
'I'll name him Bambi.'

the mother deer answered.
'Bambi.'
Bambi.
Bam  bi.
Bam  bi Lamp.
I have a Bambi Lamp.
I found it.
It's mine.

CURTAIN

# Justice Takes A Roadtrip

© 1996 Anita Loomis

*[Anita is on the lip, stage right. She gets down on her hands and knees and places a matchbox-sized white Bronco truck in front of her. She crawls, slowly pushing the toy across the stage, as she speaks.]*

**ANITA:**

There are eighteen women waiting in the state of Illinois. Waiting for a pardon, one each.

I don't know their names.

Maybe four used knives, maybe nine used guns, one might have used poison, Drano or bleach, one might have used a pillow if she was big enough and he was drunk enough, two might have hired help if they had a little cash, the last one could have left her baby at her sister's and gone home with enough rage to keep hitting him with the baseball bat he so lately used on her.

I don't know their blood types, their DNA, their glove sizes, their alleged whereabouts at the times of the murders. I don't know whether they have dandruff, bad knees or previous records of police intervention in situations of domestic violence.

I don't know if any of them are pretty.

They'd like to get of jail, they say. It was self-defense, they say. It was him or me, they say. One of them might have said she wouldn't let him stick her head in the toilet one more time.

I don't know what they say.

Eighteen women waiting for someone to excuse them their behavior, to absolve them of their anger, to forgive them all their rage.

Eighteen women waiting. I don't know anything about them.

Why should I believe them? I don't even know their names.

*[She pushes the toy car off the edge of the stage.]*

CURTAIN

# Fairy Tale for When
# the Cupboard Is Bare

© 1996 Ayun Halliday

[*Ayun sits on a high stool in a very small spotlight. The vocal and emotional sensibility of this play is as dull and unvaried as possible, with just a touch of anxiety. Enthusiasm may be betrayed only on the line "He was smuggling something!"*]

**AYUN:**

Once upon a time there were five teenaged warriors. One of the warriors was named Tim and he wore a blue unitard. One of the warriors was named Kelly and she wore a purple unitard. One of the warriors was named Marty and he wore a yellow unitard. One of the warriors was named Zach and he wore a green unitard. One of the warriors was named Steph and she wore a pink unitard. A warrior is a person who knows karate and fights bad guys. Warriors smell good and say no to drugs. A unitard is a stretchy cat suit. You have to be thin to wear a unitard. Warriors are thin. The warriors had a mascot. The mascot was a dog-shaped robot named Squeaks who said things like "Uh-oh!" and "Go, warriors!" A robot is an old-fashioned computer. Squeaks is funny because in real-life, dogs do not talk. If you buy a Squeaks doll, you will have to use your imagination to make him talk. You can have him say things like "Uh-oh!" and "Go, warriors!" One day, the warriors heard about a bad guy named Xavier. He was smuggling something! Xavier had two AK-47s, a Sigma 3, a sawed off shotgun and a deer hunting rifle with a custom muzzle. He blew some guy's hand off, but it looked totally fake. He had sex with a lady and she was naked. Then he had sex with another lady and then he said, "Bitch, you trying to fuck me over?" and he blew a hole in her stomach and he said "Eat this," and it looked totally real because you could see her guts. Guts are organs that are inside our bodies and when they are injured, it is an excruciatingly painful experience that frequently ends in death. Death is when you stop breathing and you have no pulse. Xavier had a suitcase full of money. Then the warriors kicked through the wall and karate chopped him. Huh! Huh! Huh! And Squeaks said, "Uh-oh, warriors, here comes trouble!" and Freddy Krueger came and went uh-uh-uh with his hands and the warriors were all bloody and stuff and they died. Freddy Krueger is

**70**

scary because in real-life men do not have knives for fingers. Except Freddy Krueger won't scare you, unless you are some kind of baby. Freddy Krueger caught Squeaks and went uh-uh-uh and Squeaks was dead too and then Freddy Krueger was the king and he lived happily ever after and stuff.

CURTAIN

# Former Firefighter's Slide Show #1: A Beautiful Sunday Morning

© 2000 Marjorie Fitzsimmons

[*There is a slide projector but no slides. When Marjorie requests the next slide, the slide carousel advances, but every screen is white light. Marjorie reacts and gestures, as though the pictures described are being projected.*]

**MARJORIE:**

First slide please, Bob.

Here we are at the firehouse #3 when we first got the call. We thought it was going to be this cab driver who'd been missing for about a month so we were really worried that he'd be all bloaty and rotten with parts eaten off but as it turned out, it wasn't him.

Next slide, please.

Okay, here's the body floating face down in the Elk River. See the exit wound on the back?

Next slide.

Here's the body being turned over. I think we were all more shocked that it had breasts than that her throat had been slashed from ear to ear. Look how red the water got. We later found out that she was some crack whore.

Bob?

And here we are cruising down the river to the dock where the ambulance was waiting. It took a while. You can see me there in the front of the pontoon boat beside that big blue tarp. She was under there. See her arm sticking out? Just enough rigor mortis had set in, the coroner said she'd been dead about 24 hours, that her arm kept popping out from under there. I kept putting it back in but it kept popping back out.

Next slide, please.

Here's a boater who waved and smiled at us as we passed by. All the boaters we passed that morning waved and smiled. I waved but I wasn't able to smile. She waved sometimes too. Then I'd put her arm back under.

Okay, Bob.

Oh, here's the captain in the back of the boat trying to get away from the smell. It wasn't unbearable. I didn't feel I could leave her side so I stayed up front.

All right.

This is me with the paramedic at the dock zipping her into the body bag. We had to force it a little, but not much. That arm.

Next.

Here we are back at the station. The other firefighters are alternately checking to see if I'm doing okay and accusing me of being a dead body magnet. I ended up getting a reputation for that.

Last slide, please.

Now they're saying, aren't you sorry you worked overtime today and I think to myself—No. No. I'm not sorry. I'm glad I was there to take care of her.

CURTAIN

# Vision

**HEATHER:**

Here. Here I cannot see you. And you know what that means—out of sight, out of mind. You are gone to me, because I do not see you, because I choose not to see you.

Because you are not here, you are not.

Even if you stood here (and please, please, don't, but even if you did) I would move you, move you out of my plane of vision, cut you out of the picture. I would turn around, or turn my head, or, not wanting to expend the effort, my tiny, delicate ocular muscles would choose to move past this distraction of the past that is all you mean to me now, and focus on something clear and bright and something that is not you. Or I can close my eyes and see you how I would like you to be, in my mind's eye—fading, vanishing, just barely a memory.

Here you are not.

CURTAIN

# Untitled (measurement piece)

© 2000 Connor Kalista

[*There are three scoop lights on the floor, each in their own area of the stage. The play begins in blackout. Connor turns on first scoop. There is an apple here.*]

**CONNOR:**
One for Tom, who kissed me three times.

[*Connor takes three bites of the apple and replaces it in front of the light. Connor turns on second scoop. There is a ream of paper here. Connor silently counts out 38 sheets of paper and lays these next to the original stack.*]

One for Felix, who was thirty-eight years old.

[*Connor turns on third scoop. There is a ball of twine and pair of scissors here. Connor stretches a length of twine from his toe to just below his shoulders.*]

One for David, who is five foot six.

[*Connor cuts this length of twine and exits.*]

CURTAIN

# He's Got The Whole World (or a minor portion of the population thereof) In His Hand

© 1995 Stephanie Shaw

**STEPHANIE:**

All right, look, I pull my weight. I just like to sleep and I don't get much done in the morning, that's all. I am not fully functioning in the morning, OK? That's just the way it is and Mr. Efficient has just got to live with it.

Not that he says anything, mind you. It's just implicit. He makes me breakfast. He brings me my coffee. I mean, my God, what am I supposed to make of that? I can only assume it's all part of his master design to make me look bad in my own home. Like I need any help looking bad at seven-thirty a.m., with a basal thermometer sticking out of my mouth and a handful of charts tracking my ovulation and no real urge to fuck whether it's baby time or not because at seven-thirty in the morning I feel about as sexy as a yeast infection.

And while I waste a whole day stressing over whether we'll ever get pregnant or not, he calmly cleans the cat box, puts new tires on the car, finishes his master's thesis, does the laundry, kills a mastodon, and cooks dinner. Sometimes I wish he'd just cut it out. The only time he sits still longer than me is when he's on the toilet.

And now, in the wake of my sorry reproductive history, I send him off to get a sperm count and he comes back with some interesting but hardly surprising news.

[*Addressing an audience member:*] Do you know how many sperm— per squirt—are required to make a man fertile? Guess. 20 million. My husband, the overachiever, produces *240 million sperm per average ejaculate*. 240 million. Let me demonstrate.

[*Pulls out bottle of creme hair conditioner and squirts a white viscous puddle of it on the stage floor.*]

That, right there, 240 million sperm.

That's nearly the equivalent of the population of the United States of America!

And he's carrying it around in his balls.

I knew he was twice a valedictorian, I had no idea that he was also a Spermidictorian.

I live with The Sperminator.

Spermy the Clown.

My clown. My perfect spermy clown.

CURTAIN

# Bewitched Bothered and Bewildered

*[David stands, arms outstretched, a heavy book resting in each palm.]*

**DAVID:**

Elizabeth Montgomery has died. She had rectal cancer. You won't read about that in *Newsweek Magazine.* People don't want to know about that. Rectal cancer. Elizabeth Montgomery once played a witch on TV. Samantha. I have a niece named Samantha. My brother and his wife named their child after a TV character. They've always liked the name. Elizabeth Montgomery didn't like playing the witch really. But the show was very camp. Paul Lynde and Agnes Moorehead were on the show. Paul Lynde was in the center square on *Hollywood Squares.* He was as out and outrageous as he could be then. Agnes Moorehead was a closeted lesbian who had a crush on Susan Hayward. Susan Hayward and Agnes Moorehead died of cancer most likely brought on by being in a very bad movie made on a nuclear test site in the 1950s. On the show Agnes Moorehead dressed like a drag queen. Today, men in drag sometimes dress like Agnes Moorehead. Elizabeth Montgomery didn't really like being on the show. She wanted to be a serious actress. She played Lizzie Borden in a movie once. *The Legend of Lizzie Borden* the movie is called. There is speculation that the real Lizzie Borden was a lesbian. *The Legend of Lizzie Borden* did not bring up this speculation. In the movie when I saw it for the first time as an ABC movie of the week I noticed a sign in the window. IRISH KEEP OUT. I wondered why that was. At that time I was not aware of Irish prejudice in 19th century America. I asked my history teacher, Mr. Lamb, about the sign. He told me not to believe anything I see on TV. And especially in movies like *The Legend of Lizzie Borden.* And the class laughed. I found out about Irish prejudice in 19th century America on my own. It made me realize that I shouldn't believe everything I learn in history class, especially history class taught by Mr. Lamb. During those middle years of school I was as gay as Paul Lynde, Agnes Moorehead and Lizzie Borden. Like Lizzie Borden and Agnes Moorehead and Paul Lynde I acted up. Mr. Lamb made me stand in front of the class holding books in my outstretched arms like this as punishment one day for bad behavior. When Elizabeth Montgomery died of rectal cancer I thought of how embarrassed Mr. Lamb made me feel. I remembered the weight of those books.

CURTAIN

# The Pitter-Pat of Tiny Feet

© 1993 Greg Allen

**GREG:**

I had a baby last week.

We did, my wife and I.

For about twelve hours until the pregnancy test came back negative.

Yes, we had a baby the minute Miriam woke up sick, throwing up into the toilet—which at first was cause for sympathy and concern, but on second thought became a sign, a symbol of something yet to come, a tangible manifestation of an eight pound six ounce bouncing baby boy named Noah or Abraham (girl's names yet to be announced) drooling on my shoulder and spitting up in a much cuter way than his mother was now bent gagging over the porcelain throne.

Yes, one little stream of vomit and our lives were irrevocably changed. After all, we had been talking about "when" and "how" and "where" just the other morning, but now that Miriam's puking we don't even have to plan the damn thing! To say nothing of "trying" to get pregnant, like so many couples talk about "trying" to get pregnant for months and months and months—which does sound like fun—but think of the anxiety, anxiety which is now eliminated because the bathroom is resonating with the SACRED CRYPTIC SONG OF THE GODS! A veritable beacon! An angel's cry! A (choking) HALLELUJAH, A CHILD IS BORN! on this day (in nine months) and this home will be graced with a babe wrapped in bohemian clothes and crying in a manner which will wake us up at all hours of the night yearning for life-giving sustenance and love and warmth and attention and knowledge and experience of the world and protection from the evil that lurks in the hearts of men!

A little screaming presence to quiet and coddle, to teach to say "Dad" and "Mom" and "Neo-Futurarium."

To put one foot in front of the other to crawl and walk and run.

To put on a bike and send off into the world...and bandage his head-wounds when he comes back.

To show how to tackle any challenge that stands in his way, whether it takes the form of societal injustice or a bully with a baseball bat. To never bend to the whips of conformity nor the whims of inhibition. To say "Dad, I want the car keys. I'm going out on a date and I may not come home!"

To have every experience from mountain climbing in the Alps to major hallucinogens in the alley.
To have all the power and joy and self-confidence that I had—
HAVE! ...Have.

And then the test came back negative.

And although part of me was sad that somewhere a little idea of a child died, I was also relieved to have at least a few more months where I was just responsible for *my*self and *my* life.

. Where a cry was just a cry, and where throwing up was just gross—and nothing more.

CURTAIN

[*NOTE: The word "Neo-Futurarium" can be replaced with any polysyllabic word you choose to add local color.*]

# Before we are to sleep tonight, you should know more.

[*Robert stands on stage with an easel holding placards. As Robert delivers the text the placards are presented one at a time revealing his sexually history, so that the last placard is revealed just before the end of the text is delivered. (E.g. 'Do you know him?' 'This is Rob.' 'He is 27.' 'Rob is not a virgin.' 'Rob 1st had sex when he was 17.' 'On New Year's Eve.' 'Since then Rob has had sex with 24 women & 0 men.' 'Three times the condom has broken.' 'Rob has had sex without a condom.' 'She was a virgin. He wasn't.' 'Two times he was tested for HIV,' 'and the results were negative.' 'He is waiting for the results of his 3rd test.' 'From the New York City Department of Health.' 'Do you know him?' 'This is Rob.')*]

**ROB:**
No matter the weather;
No matter.
These are not the gray days.
No, nor the raining days of solitude.
Here is a time of adoration and honor.
Praise is not lost;
Praise is not found;
It is given,
    And I know I am in tow
    troubled by the many nasty dishes to be done,
    troubled by the daily tasks that slip quickly between digits,
    troubled for tuning the telephone to know your call
    and many times hearing nothing.

But deeds are not seen as wrong, just misjudged or misjuggled,
At times.

At times.
I have waited for you to ring;
I have waited cold alone outside the stained glass;
I have waited watching the rain pelt bounding squirrels
    directly in the eyes.

**81**

I have waited.
I have.
I know you have.
At times.

I know
You too
Have.

Laughing;
We laugh bringing
   laugh upon laugh,
   smile upon smile,
   a tricky love upon table cloths
   of black and white checks.

Kept mute before our relatives.
Who greedily eat expecting regularity,
as if served endless platters of pasta.

We drink tasting wines not found in cellars or casks,
But wines of our ancestors; wines of past masteries.

We eat from foundations that will not fall when the table is knocked by
drunken cousin or dog no matter how much either has had to drink.

We think we see choices resonating in each other's face;
Not wise but more mature,
   more nurture,
   more natural
   We breathe
Mighty in combination
   for piety is not beneath us
   it is encompassing.

Having brought this to you,
I wring my hands and
    blue sensations float across my finger tips.
I cry in that things will change;
I cry.
I sing in that things will last;
I sing.
I live in that
    little place there, that
    only you can find, that
    special little place molded out of sand and sea water,
    that place is where I really live,
    only there,
    for what we have,
I live.

CURTAIN

# Foretold

[*Rachel is standing in the theater doorway, illuminated by a very strong backlight. Offstage there is the amplified noise of someone hitting something hollow, maybe a box, at excruciating intervals. Also the noise of something scratchy and heavy being dragged across the floor and bundles of sticks being snapped; things breaking periodically that shouldn't.*]

**RACHEL:**

In this city, says the prophet, in this city everything and everyone is burning. People burn in the streets and the streets are ash. Nobody can drive anymore because the guardrails look as though your teeth might drag against them as you raced past, your teeth shrieking on steel, your skin interrupted by the concrete.

In this city, says the prophet, no one has use for a weapon, everything and everyone is a knife trying to sharpen themselves against the sky, so the sky sucked itself into itself, went rigid like a lover who refuses to be kissed and now the sky, the ground, and the people, they all throw sparks, they shear and spit, catch on each other and whine and grind like bad machinery, trying to say something that will always sound like a mistake.

Here is why, says the prophet, why is that there was one angel, and she lived in the chest of a statue of a man on a hill in the park in the city. Every morning she would pound with her fists on the chest of the statue and it would make a terrible noise, she would do it just to remind the people that she was there but everyone thought it was the blood pounding in their ears and it only reminded them of sleep, of tired, of sick, how they really should be lying down, how they really should stop and when they stopped, they saw the statue unfold his arms and set her free, and she wasn't an angel, she was just a girl with a bad cough and seeing this, seeing her stumble away, all the people knew they had a secret, a secret that was too much, that burned them up, made the sky go wrong and the girl, she walks with a black tongue and a cigarette and she laughs because it's all a joke, isn't it, the joke is that you can't ask anyone who's on fire for a light, everyone here is burning and you can't even smoke, says the prophet, how funny is that, she says, how funny is that?

[*There is the sound of all doors in the theater being slammed one after the other ending with the door in which Rachel is standing.*]

CURTAIN

# I Need A Shower

© 1999 Marjorie Fitzsimmons

[*Marjorie sits at a table with bridal registry from Target and an Aunt Jemima spatula.*]

**MARJORIE:**

I'm making a list. A list of things that I want other people to buy me. I was at a bridal shower the other day and decided I deserved to be showered. I'm never going to get married. Who else thinks it's a distinct possibility that they will never get married? See. OK. Who thinks it may be a long time before you get married? OK. What do you do in the meantime? Aren't you as an individual just as deserving as those about to be married? Plus it makes sense to give stuff to an individual. I'm not going to break up with me. [*To audience member:*] You're not going to break up with you. You're too nice, right, and you're great in bed. No nasty battle over who gets the Cuisinart. You get the Cuisinart. My way is better, simpler, cleaner. I want stuff and I know what I want. I don't have to hash it out with somebody else. I'm sick of using the spatula that came out of the Aunt Jemima Pancake mix. [*Whips out said spatula and wields it.*] I want that shiny, silver, German shit. I could buy it—but I don't want to!

People who are getting married register. They get exactly what they fucking want. They tell people where to buy it, what kind, the size, the color, and the quantity. I find that incredibly brazen for anyone over the age of ten. Every Christmas I would make a detailed list of exactly what I wanted and I'd end up getting a bunch of crap I didn't want. I got stupid baby dolls out the butt, but I never got the ventriloquist dummy or the bow and arrow set or the metal detector. Well, this time it's going to be different. [*Whacks table with spatula, stands on table.*] I'm registered at Target. Marjorie Fitzsimmons and No Body. I'm old and I need stuff. Just buy me whatever I fucking tell you, you cheap bastards. You all know I'm a big ol' dyke so give me what I want and I won't kick your ass. Me, me, me, it's all about me. [*Jumps off table.*]

CURTAIN

# A brief reminder
# of my place here with you

**GERYLL:**

Today I am Black.

Right now I am as Black as
the darkest new moon night
on a back woods country road.

Earlier I was Brown
and another day or
perhaps even later
tonight
High Yella—

But right now,
at this very moment—

As the only, or one of the few chips in this vanilla cookie
that I choose to
bear my soul
share my wisdom or lack thereof,
I am a nigger witnessing to the power of myself as other.

Attempting to find
within our differences
a place so personal
that its breath can be heard by all the people who care to listen
to the testament of my
one/singleness
here
with you.

I am aware.
I am sometimes angry to be here alone.
I am often embarrassed to be here
alone.
I need this moment
to remember

*[Long pause as Geryll makes eye contact with as many people as possible.]*

I am not here...
alone.

CURTAIN

# Apprehension Of Pretension

**SCOTT:**

For fear of being wordy
I wrote this little play

I wrote it with some little words
that all can easy say

I wrote it at my little desk
I wrote it in a rhyme

I wrote with some special care
I wrote it IN SHORT TIME

I wanted you to know that
although we take great care

that all we do is clear to you
that all is just and fair

sometimes we are too clever
sometimes we are too flip

sometimes we write about ourselves
sometimes we cannot successfully execute our intentions to the degree
that will be pleasurable, for both us and the recipients of our message,
that is to say, the audience, via mimesis to achieve the desired cathartic
—oh shit!

[*Walks off stage.*]

CURTAIN

# For You Only

© 1994 Greg Kotis

[*Greg Kotis sits center stage. He delivers the following monologue to a single audience member, still seated in the audience, by speaking to him/her through a "tin-can-phone."*]

**GREG:**

I wanted to write a play about my first kiss. About being fifteen. About memories which stay with you all your life like snapshots in a wallet. About love, I guess, and remembering. Here it is. [*Pause.*]

Her name was Beth and she had long brown hair and chipped front teeth, deep green eyes and a pug nose. She was short and muscular and she ran track and one day she invited me to a party which my father had to drive me to. I had been warned beforehand by my brother's best friend that she "liked" me, as we used to say, and that I better be ready for something. I was ready, in a way, but not in a particularly useful way. I was afraid, and at the party I concentrated on taking every last piece of paper and glue off the bottle of beer I held. So here's what she did. When the party was at its fullest she sat down next to me and watched me peel for awhile. Then she took the bottle away from me, took my hand, and led me into the room where all the coats were. Then she closed the door, sat me down on the coats, and sat down beside me. Then she took my head in her hands and leaned toward me and pulled me toward her. Then her lips parted a little and I could see where her teeth were chipped. Then she touched her lips to mine and pressed her lips to mine and kissed me for a very long time until I realized that I was kissing her, too. And then she moved her mouth to my ear and started following the path of my ear with her tongue, and I remember thinking, "I've never heard anything like this before." The sound was strange and soothing and very nice, clicking and clacking and breathing and warm. And then I said something stupid because I was afraid. I said, "I bet you do this with all the—" But she stopped me because she knew I was afraid and didn't want me to be stupid, too. She cupped her hands to my ear and whispered, "For you, only, Greg. Only for you." Then the door opened and my brother's best friend looked in and smiled and said, "Look at little Kotis." But I didn't hear him.

CURTAIN

# Fuck You, Bruno Bettelheim

© 1997 Stephanie Shaw

*[Stephanie tells a story, holding a book with illustrations by David Kodeski.]*

**STEPHANIE:**

Once upon a time there was a brother and a sister who were put out into the woods because their father was poor and the stepmother convinced him that his two kids ate too much, *and maybe she was right*, but even if she wasn't he probably would've done it anyway because he was clearly what would be called pussy-whipped—no other explanation.

Gretel is a young lady of peculiar intensity, not necessarily a physical beauty you understand, but strikingly manic depressive which can be very attractive under the right circumstances.

Hansel is purely beautiful. If anyone is going to be caged and fattened for food, it is going to be him.

They sit in the dark wood and hold hands.

They wander, oral fixation never satisfied, until they come upon the house of gingerbread. They fall on it, sucking on shingles, licking at lattices, tuck-pointing with their tongues, the termites.

You want to warn her. The witch. You want to say "Don't invite them in. One will seduce you, the other will murder you."

But, oh, Hansel is so delicious. What old woman would not invite him in for flapjacks?

What makes this old woman a witch? Her lust for his flesh, his youth? Her urge to devour him; to swallow whole his calm strength, his boyish piety, the spice of his self-righteousness? Who would not want to devour him? We are all capable. We act it out in metaphors.

Unless we are Gretel. If anyone is capable of putting an old woman in a stove, it is her. She does not pause to think about what the fire will do to the tough old woman; the screams, the smell, the popping of tendons as the flames spring them from their casings. Gretel, manic, reaches in after the old woman's heart and eats it only slightly roasted, burning her lips with it.

90

Hansel watches, beautiful boy in a cage, and wonders if the evil old heart will cure his sister. The salts in that diabolical engine might balance her. Depressed, Gretel would have had barely the strength to drag herself into the oven and close the door after her. To lay down in the heat and close her eyes before the lids fried off and they melted like eggs sunny-side up into her head.

The witch would not touch her. You don't eat a mad dog. You don't eat gingerbread houses and you don't eat poison apples and you don't open certain doors that appeal or marry men with tinted beards, you should embrace amphibians but avoid exceedingly hairy types and you shouldn't trust ugly people but you'd better damn well be nice to them.

The end.

CURTAIN

# The Ghoul

[*Blackout. Scott lights a candle.*]

**SCOTT:**
My father is a ghoul. Even as we speak, my father waits for someone like you to die. My father imagines horrible things happening to you, people like you. My father wishes that you will drink too much and operate heavy machinery. My father hopes that you will wear your hat the wrong way in the wrong part of town. My father is desirous that you meet a quick, violent death within easy access of a first-class medical facility, so that highly trained men and women may carefully remove that fleshly bellows, that spidery network of capillaries, bronchi and alveoli, that one good lung, lovingly pack it in ice and fly it to the hills of North Carolina. There, specialists in the arcane arts will place it in my father's chest so that he may live, he may live, he may live. In Rio de Janeiro, they would not wait. They would simply drive into the slums, and kill some street urchin, and keep killing until they found the right blood type. We, however, live in a more civilized society, and so we must wait. My father and I are waiting for someone like you to die. We are ghouls, my father and I, we are ghouls.

[*Scott blows out candle.*]

CURTAIN

# El-oquence

**MARJORIE:**

She was on the El. Five feet tall and tan, not a tooth in her head. She wore a red coat, rotting tennis shoes and a garbage bag for a skirt. And this is what she said without taking a breath.

"So what happens? You're a bully, a faggot. What is justice, what is right, what is wrong? I'll rip your bleached blonde hair out by its motherfucking roots. Bitch, cunt, try me. A citation, just like a traffic ticket and they laugh. Eight hours of community service. That's what the bitch says, plead guilty. They give you a choice man. Fuck, shit. Sit your ass down ho. Try me. I'll kick your ass, try me. Say it again and I'll kick your ass. Go home and fuck your wife's cunt. Shit. Try me."

I wonder what she meant by that?

CURTAIN

# FROGS!!!

**SEAN:**

I have this fear that if there is such a thing as reincarnation, I'll come back as a frog and suffer the same stupid, inhumane cruelties my friends and I inflicted on them. Things I cannot even breathe out loud. Sick, prepubescent, Nazi-esque things. I was only twelve at the time and have no other excuse.

Five years later, when I was 17, I did another stupid, inhumane thing. This time to myself. I joined the Army. But I only lasted three months because of those frogs.

See, I fell asleep one night in my foxhole while we were playing war games and I dreamed. I dreamed about my worst fear coming true. When I woke up, it was raining. My foxhole was half-filled with mud and water and I was green. My fatigues covered my body in woodland green and my hands and face were covered in shades of green camouflage make-up. I had to search for my true skin color. The only part of me left white was my belly.

I crawled out of the foxhole—out of the water and onto the land. A flare lit up the sky. I heard the gunfire and I saw the helicopters coming. Like screaming hoards of blood hungry twelve year old sadists. And me a frog. Instant-karma.

CURTAIN

# The Pieces of My Self That Have Accrued Like Belly Button Crust in One Minute or Less

© 2001 Genevra Gallo

*[Genevra asks the audience for someone who has a watch with a second hand and requests that they time her for one minute; if "time" is called before the end of the monologue, Genevra must stop.]*

**GENEVRA:**

I have trouble remembering to floss. I like to eat the green M&Ms because my mother and I both have green eyes and those were the most important ones when we ate them together in my childhood. I have three tattoos. I love them all. I believe that tattooing is, in fact, a modern-day, westernized scarification ritual whose necessity was brought on by the backlash to the loss of a clear, moral, and stable adult presence in the lives of children born in the early seventies. I love kids. Chocolate chip cookies, without nuts, are—without argument—the best cookie ever invented. I think Nick Park is a genius. I miss Jim Henson, and I hate the fact that the new Muppet show sucks and that later generations will never understand why all the Gen X-ers in the world won't let go of a frog, a pig, and some singing chickens. I have finally been convinced of the superiority of Macintosh, and while I still don't consider Bill Gates the devil, my boyfriend is at least temporarily pleased with my conversion. I believe that we are still living in a society created, controlled, and dominated by white, Christian men. I am fascinated by the Rosie-the-Riveter phenomenon and particularly by the subsequent propagandizing of women like June Cleaver and Harriet Nelson in the country's desperate attempt to convince women that they would be more beautiful and valuable if they gave up their new-found independence and opted for vacuums and baking instead. I am pro-choice. I can't decide what I want to be "when I grow up." I never understood the popularity of Nell Carter. I believe Paul Simon is a great poet. I no longer kill spiders. I actually do hug trees. I can tell how long a relationship will last in the first two seconds of the first kiss. I believe I will never truly understand why I am here.

*[Either time is called or the monologue is finished, at which point Genevra takes the watch and says:]*

Okay. Now it's your turn. It works exactly the same way.

[*She gets the audience member to do the same for one minute (ramble on about themselves without thinking or stopping) until time is called or they run out of steam.*]

CURTAIN

# 30 Seconds Of Life

*[In the dark Diana calls "30 Seconds Of Life, Go!" She starts a stopwatch. Steve lights John's face with a scoop light. John opens his eyes.]*

**JOHN:**

I am alive. I've just opened the eyes of the speaker speaking me, and I see you watching. And it feels right. There is not enough time to get to know each and every one of you, and this I regret. But I do want to thank you for being around to hear the words that have borrowed this voice. I need to remind you of the beauty that some of you may have begun to take for granted, the endless possibilities of the world that surrounds. There are loves to experience with unavoidable accidents and pains you'll have to endure. But it's worth it, my friends. I am just these words. I am as long as the length of this play. I existed only for you. Please take the time out to stare at a tree. Say 'Hello' to someone who is crying. Sit still and listen to music...

**DIANA:**

Time's up!

*[Steve says, "CURTAIN" and then turns off the scoop light.]*

*[NOTE: The time usually expires before John says, "listen to music," but if it hasn't, John continues giving examples of the beautiful things we could do with the moments of every single day.]*

# One Night With Elvis

[*Steve sits on stage with a boom box playing an Elvis tune... preferably old Elvis..."Mystery Train." He turns it down as he begins to speak.*]

**STEVE:**

"I hate Elvis!" my mother said as we drove together listening to "The King" on the radio. I had heard this before from her but never with an explanation. I had always assumed it was just because she hated rock and roll. But this time she clarified what I considered her sacrilegious statement. She told me when she was growing up and Elvis was first drafted into the army Elvis made the comment that he refused to stay in the barracks with any Mexicans. As we drove on, my allegiance to the king now in question, we crossed into the city of Whittier, a small city on the East Side of Los Angeles, close to where I grew up. Both of my sisters now own homes there with their families. My mother continued on over Elvis and told me about the city of Whittier, and how when she was growing up Mexicans were only allowed there to work. To wash dishes in some of the restaurants or to clean and groom some of the well kept middle-class homes. And if any Mexicans were caught in Whittier after sunset they were either beaten, thrown in jail or both. "That's how things were back then when I was growing up," she said. I looked over at her, trying not to be too obvious...her face staring straight ahead at the familiar streets leading up to my sisters' brand new homes. Her face looked a little sad but I could almost see a brief hint of pride each time a street light flashed inside the car. As we continued on through the quaint narrow streets and small Monopoly-like houses of Whittier, I remember reaching down and tuning the radio to a different station...I think it was classical.

CURTAIN

# It's all about attainable goals in the '01

[*Chloë takes out a stuffed frog, throws it on the ground, takes a deep breath, leaps over it. Repeats twice. Picks up the frog, kisses him; he doesn't turn into a prince. She gets ready to jump over him again.*]

*CURTAIN*

# And Then There Was Geryll: A Creation Story.

© 1996 Geryll Robinson

[*Geryll is discovered on the floor in near darkness. The following is spoken in a desperate stage whisper. The voices are optional or can be spoken by the same actor performing the monologue if she is creative.*]

**GERYLL:**

Once upon a time upon a once upon a nice—lady—olden days long time before me lady—white lady—young lady, olden days lady—before there was me before there was air lady. Nice lady olden days lady once upon a white lady young nice confused...lady

**VOICES:**

Your MOTHER.

**GERYLL:**

Mother—mine knew a man—young man. Two man. Old man. Old man young man. Young man like young lady—young white lady like young white man. Plus and until old not young not white old man not young lady meet old man somewhere in old man in the shadows. Old man young lady young man. Young lady question. Young lady wants. Young man is white young man is in darkness. Black old man in the shadows old black man in shadows with with—this is was difficult for telling old black man in shadows with...young white lady. Wow—secret! Young man is in darkness—Young lady in shadows of old black man—with old black man sssssshhhhhhshhhhhshhhhshhhh. Old black man. Man in shadows old man—is, is, is...

**VOICES:**

Your daddy.

**GERYLL:**

Daddy—not that Hanson young man Tommy Hanson not Hanson—Mr. Hanson—young white man in darkness thinks "here comes baby—here comes baby my baby. Hanson baby. My little white happy Hanson baby."

**VOICES:**

Black baby.

**GERYLL:**

Black baby. Bring the black man old man out of shadows black man use the shadows black man use the light Black man get your black baby young lady old man young lady black baby old man young lady get your black baby, kiss your black baby, love your black baby in the light.

[*Lights slowly rise on Geryll.*]

CURTAIN

# I'M GOING TO GIVE THIS TO THE GUY SLEEPING ON THE BENCH OUTSIDE

[*Bill walks on stage.*]

**BILL:**

If there is anyone who would like to participate in the next play, would you please hold either a dollar or a quarter above your head. Thank you.

[*Neo-Futurists gather the participants on to the stage. The participants are to hold the money above their heads even when on stage. When all participants are on stage, their money is collected in a bag. They are then rushed out of the theater to find the first person they see sleeping on a bench, or on the street. The person who is sleeping is awakened, and asked if they would like the money collected by the surrounding group of people. The group is then led back to the theater. While this whole event is happening, the audience still left in the theater are listening to a recording of testimonials from homeless men and women. That or Neil Diamond music. "CURTAIN" is called when everyone has returned to their seat.*]

# Oma

*[Greg stands on stage and addresses the audience. The "voice" is done in Greg's best impression of Oma—a German Jewish woman in her eighties.]*

**GREG:**

I used to live with my friend Billy Jonas. And the phone would occasionally ring, and this voice would say:

> "'Ello? Iz Beely dare?"

And I'd say "No he's not, can I take a message?" And the voice would say:

> "Thees iz Beely's Oma. Do you know what an Oma iz?"

And I'd say "Yeah, hi Oma, how are you..." But she'd go on and say:

> "Thees iz Beely's Grandmutter. An Oma iz a Grandmutter. Beely never calls me. I worry about him..."

And I had learned that, but every time I answered the phone she would ask:

> "Do you know what an Oma iz?"

Well now I live with Miriam Whiteley, and the phone occasionally rings and... there's this voice:

> "Hello. Iz Miriam dare?"

And I'd say "No, no she's not..." And the voice would say:

> "Thees iz Miriam's Oma. Do you know what an Oma iz?"

And I'd go "Yeah, hi Oma, how are you..." And she'd say:

> "Thees iz Miriam's Grandmutter. An Oma iz a Grandmutter. Miriam never calls me. I worry about her..."

And I started to think—"Could this be the same woman?" I mean, I know Billy and Miriam aren't related in any way, but...maybe there's just like this one giant Oma out there who calls everyone's roommate and insists that we don't know who they are.

Well, finally I got a chance to meet Oma at Sue, Miriam's mom's, house. And she was exactly as I pictured her—short, and old, and feisty, and she had this gray wig slapped on the top of her head. And we were walking down the hall with all these old family pictures in it, and she stopped me and pointed to a picture of a woman with a young child, and she said:

"Thees iz Sue when she was a leettle girl."

And I said "Oh, and is this woman you, Oma?" And she said:

"No. That's Sue's Oma. She died in the camp. We watched my husband starve to death and my father was gassed."

And I thought, "No. I don't know what an Oma is."

CURTAIN

[*NOTE: The dialect fades away during Oma's last two lines.*]

# Phantom Pain

[*Ayun stands balanced on one foot, holding the other foot behind her to create the appearance of a missing lower limb.*]

**AYUN:**

Something happens when you lose a leg. You can still feel pain in the foot that's not there. Your brain lies to you, says, "I'm sorry to have to be the one to break it to you, but that leg's gone for good," and then it sneaks around behind your back to lay out a pair of slippers. I wouldn't know. I have both my legs and mostly, I forget to feel them at all. It's easy to forget. I forget and think I'll see you behind the plate glass window of a certain restaurant. And that your hair will be the same. I remember when today is your birthday and every time I hear the words "Venice Beach" I pipe up, "Oh, I have friends there," meaning your sister, who, fibs my brain, cannot truthfully still be my friend. I think about your wedding which I won't go to even though I received an invitation addressed to "Miss" and how you'll remember me fondly on that special day above all your other friends and your bride and everybody and I have these thoughts because sometimes I catch my brain parading around in a hoopskirt and a dress made out of curtains and even though it insists it's just for fun, deep in some wrinkle I cannot reach, my brain truly believes it is Scarlett O'Hara. Sometimes I can almost feel your coat and then I realize it's not your coat at all, not the soft, sweet calfskin, but me and how I was then, a thousand miles away and crazy for you. When all I wanted was to feel that calfskin against my cheek and knew in two weeks that I would. Something happens when you lose a leg. You close your eyes and feel your foot. I wouldn't know. I forgot how much I loved those shoes.

CURTAIN

# An Apology

© 1996 Greg Allen

[*The stage is in darkness. A spotlight slowly rises to show Greg sitting in a chair. He begins quiet and sincere but becomes increasingly vehement until he is spitting black bile by the end—figuratively of course.*]

**GREG:**

I am so sorry. I am really, really so...incredibly sorry. I really cannot express how incredibly...regretful...and filled with remorse, I am. I just feel awful. I do not deserve to live, to breathe, to exist here on this plain of reality. I am worse than the lowest of the low, the absolute bottom of the abyss of filth. I am a pig. A slug. A maggot—no not even that! A larval form of dysentery! I deserve to **wallow** in my own feces! To consume the utter dregs of a huge vat of cat vomit! My legs should be removed at the hip, hacked off with a—NO! *Ground* off slowly in a counterclockwise motion by a machine propelled by gerbils! My organs should be STREWN ABOUT THE ROOM in such a way that only a highly trained medical technician might even guess that they were once belonging to the same body. My mouth should be opened and peeled back in such a way that my entire head is just a GIANT OPEN RUNNING SORE! My family should be dissected! My possessions burned! My thoughts eradicated from the spiritual world! I should die a TORMENTED, TWISTED, PAINFUL DEATH **BEFORE** I WAS EVER BORN! NO! I SHOULD LIVE **FOREVER**, AND SEE EVERYTHING I HAVE EVER HOPED FOR AND BELIEVED IN **DASHED** TO THE GROUND AND TRAMPLED UPON BY A **HUNDRED THOUSAND DANCING SINGING FRAT BOYS**!!! I should have ***nothing*** happen to me—**FOR-EVER**! NOTHING AT ALL! I SHOULD SIT IN A ROOM **FULL OF PEOPLE** DOING NOTHING WHILE EVERYONE WATCHES **ME FEEL HOW SORRY I AM**!!!

[*Long pause while everyone watches Greg feel how sorry he is. Fade to black.*]

CURTAIN

# i'm beginning to realize why peter pan lived in never never land

*[Geryll sits facing the audience and speaks slowly and deliberately in an almost monotone.]*

**GERYLL:**
It's been a very jarring experience.
Realizing that other people
Other people's lives,
have become
my people
my life.

Understand,
this not meant to be taken in the abstract–altruistic sense...
just as simple fact.

For instance:
People my mother warned me about.

Robbers—muggers—bad guys.
People to be feared and avoided
at all costs.

People from that other world

Suddenly, robbers and muggers have become people I know.
People I took baths with as a toddler.
People I see when I go places like...
home.

Guys who get shot over drug deals
and are left to bleed to death in their cars,
have seeped out of the television and movie screens
and
landed in my circle of friends.

Strange...Stranger.

Hey stranger,
20 bucks for a blow job.

This from people I have loved...
intimately.

Dreamt of growing old with.

The outside world has somehow gotten into my living room and set up camp.

The thing is...

I don't remember sending invitations
or
letting them in.

CURTAIN

# PDA

[*Diana reads from a clipboard to the audience, allowing time for them to carry out the instructions.*]

**DIANA:**

Turn to the person on your right.

Tell that person that you love them.

Turn to the person on your left.

Tell that person that you love them.

Turn to the person on your right.

Ask that person, "How can you love me and the person on your right at the same time?"

Turn to the person on your left.

Tell that person, "I don't love the person on my right in the same way that I love you."

Turn to the person on your right.

Ask that person, "What do you mean you don't love me as much as the person on your right?"

Turn to the person on your left.

Say, "I never said that!"

Turn to the person on your right.

Say, "You did so! Just now you did!"

Turn to the person on your left.

Say, "This is hardly the time to discuss this."

Turn to the person on your right.

Say, "Coward!"

Lean forward to the person in front of you.

Ask that person, "Could you keep it down please?"

Turn to the person behind you and say, "Mind your own business!"

People in the back row, turn to the person on your left and ask, "Who the hell are you talking to?"

Everyone lean forward and glare at the person to the left of the person on your left.

Lean back.

Sigh heavily.

Close your eyes.

Say, "Look, I'm sorry."

Say, "That's okay. I'm sorry, too."

Open your eyes.

Take the hand of the person on your right.

Turn to the person on your left.

Tell that person, "I love you."

Turn to the person on your right and say, "I'm not talking to you any more."

Take your hand away.

People on the ends of rows say, "I only got about half of that."

People in the front row, reply, "Tell me about it."

You now have 5 seconds to do or say anything you want to the person on your left or on your right.

5, 4, 3, 2, 1!

Everyone stare straight ahead.

[*Pause.*]

You're on your own now.

CURTAIN

# Not Me

[*Connor sits or stands on stage as the following text is heard. During the repeated line, Connor will flick a lighter, pinch his nose then extend his arms like wings. If present, Marjorie stands vaguely near or on the stage.*]

**VOICE OVER:**

This man cannot smoke, scuba dive or ride in small engine planes.

He cannot ride comfortably in a variety of cars.

He cannot yawn without feeling a dull ache just beneath his armpit.

He cannot help but think of vomit when watching others eat bananas.

He cannot say whether or not Marjorie is in this play.

This man cannot smoke, scuba dive or ride in small engine planes.

He cannot sleep on his right side anymore.

He cannot rid himself entirely of his Southern accent.

He cannot forgive three people who will remain nameless.

He cannot tell you what this play means.

This man cannot smoke, scuba dive or ride in small engine planes.

He cannot see himself in five years.

He cannot put what he reads into practice.

He cannot stand near the front in group photos.

He cannot write himself a monologue.

[*Pause. Connor flicks lighter, pinches nose then extends his arms like wings.*]

CURTAIN

# Andy Blows Off Steam About His Ex-Friend Jamie

© 1999 Andy Bayiates

*[Andy stands center in a spot light, in front of a boom-box. He plays "Mr. Ghost Goes to Town" by the John Buzon Trio, speaking the following precisely to a rhythm in the song, as if adding spoken lyrics to the instrumental.]*

**ANDY:**

So, you hate me.
You say we shouldn't be friends.
That's fine.
But tell me
I want to know what made you frigging pissy
for months
until I asked you what was up
your ass
and you said, "nothing worth discussing."

So fine. You hate me.
You say that I've been distant.
It's true.
I have.
Ever since you started acting like a baby
when you
dated my ex-girlfriend
and said
that *you* found it
very tough to handle.

Aw...

That's *my* fault.

I *see.*

Makes perfect sense.

I know
that you
"have been trying to repair this"
just like that time you told my ex I cheated on her up and down.
That helped.
It did.

It must have made you feel good.
Now she doesn't talk to me.
I'm sure that eased some tension.

I try to be understanding
Because I know that you've got these issues
but every time I allow you to
you're acting like a shit-head.
Don't tell me I'm wrong
Don't tell me you're right
'Cause I'm the only sane one.
And I'm the one who's been holding back 'Cause your ego's fucking
fragile.

Oh,

I'm sorry.

I forgot that I got mad at you
for telling Jen I cheated on her
and I "didn't love her."

I remember
you said
that all you cared about was telling the truth
moving on
and having a "very perfect relationship."

[*Off rhythm*] You know, before they turned on me I thought your
delusions were funny. But now you've sent a mass e-mail to all our
friends trying to convince them I'm an asshole. That's a riot.

[*Back to rhythm*]

Fuck you for thinking that I wanted
anything but a friend who did not
radically suck every time I opened my mouth
for the past few years
who acts like I'm insulting him every time
I offer advice or share a view on life.
As if I give a fuck that you feel fat and
lazy next to me!

Fuck you, Jamie!

[*Off rhythm, yelling*] You can suck my dick! Which I think you must have heard is bigger than yours, you insecure motherfucker!

[*Back to rhythm*]

Okay,
I'm done.
I'm feeling a little better.
But if I ever see your face again
it will get ugly.

I hope,
I pray
someone sees this and then tells you.
And let it be a warning:
I'll do this instead of email.

[*Off rhythm*] Next time it'll be a full length musical review you miserable piece of shit.

[*As music fades, spot-light fades, Andy glances around self-consciously, a little ashamed of his anger. Blackout.*]

CURTAIN

# Mondo Boxo

[*Diana is on stage with a piece of chalk. During the play she draws three boxes on the floor around her feet, each smaller than the last. She talks and draws at the same time.*]

**DIANA:**

I live in a box. I don't really live in a box, but I feel like it sometimes. Like I live in a box. In the box I don't really but do really live in is me, like I said, and all of my things. I mean all of them, from my paper clips to my bedroom furniture, and the 24 hours of every day. Every day I get a fresh 24 hours. Also in the box are all the things I have to do. When I finish a thing, I get to throw it out of the box, but only when I am completely done with it. Like my old car. I'm completely done with that. It is no longer in the box. Puberty. Not in the box. But dirty dishes? In the box. Clean dishes? In the box. It doesn't matter, they get dirty again. Pettiness? In the box. Anger? In the box. You can imagine, I think, how crowded it is in the box that I live, but don't live, in. You can see, I think, how things get in my way in there, in here. Another thing is that the hours in the box, they take up a lot of room. You wouldn't think that would be the case. You would think that the hours would diminish, or dwindle, or get thrown out of the box, but they don't. The fewer hours I have, the more room they take up. They crowd me. Make it hard to reach things, maneuver, get things done. Because everything I have to do is in the box, too. All the typing, all the memorizing, all the cleaning, all the sleeping, all the eating and shitting and breathing I have to do is right there in the box with me, and the more I have to do, the less room. I mean it's not a very big box, really. I feel really cramped. Even though I don't really live in the box I live in. I feel really cramped. Sometimes it's hard to get my breathing done, so cramped is it. And what I want to do, what I'm kind of afraid to do, can't do, is bust out of the box. I'd like to take one of those cutters that the grocery guys have and cut the box wide open. But I can't do that. All the stuff in the box would go all over the place, I might lose some of it. And besides, I don't really live in a box. Like I said.

CURTAIN

# And The Clock's Still Ticking (for David)

**HEATHER:**

I'm in love. Very much in love. Horribly, desperately in love. Smushy, kissy, mushy, gushy, gooey, goofy love. That early-in-the-relationship, miss-you-every-hour-we're-apart love. That implosion-of-egos, practically-existing-as-one-person love. That hold-you-so-tight-it's-a-wonder-no-one's-broken-a-rib, multi-orgasmic, superlative sex, love. Happy, happy, happy. Love, love, love.

And it can't last forever, not like this, I know it can't. I mean, this relationship could last forever, we could stay together forever, we talk about being together forever, but we can't possibly maintain this much touchy-feely, lovey-dovey, everything's perfect, get 5 hours of sleep because you can't stop staring at each other, state of bliss forever. I know eventually I will need a day alone, apart. At some point I'll stop ignoring my friends. I will eventually take a shower by myself again. Or, it could be a disagreement, what if we had a difference of opinion about something. Or what if I did something, what if I did something horrible, what if I farted in his presence—I mean eventually that's going to happen—and then this perfect happiness will be over, it can't last, and it will drive me crazy, this being so happy, wondering how and when and why it will end, when it all comes crashing down around me.

But for now I'm happy.

Happy, happy, happy.

Love, love, love.

CURTAIN

# If I Were a Better Man

**JOHN:**

If I were a better Man,

I'd take my Mother out to dinner twice a week.

I'd visit my grandfather's grave and talk to him until the sun sank below the Horizon.

If I were a better man,

I'd donate half my free time to a worthy cause.

If I were a better man,

I'd run for President.

And then,

If I were president of the United States,

I'd fire all Presidential Hairstylists and Beauticians and hire a panel of some of the world's most intelligent economists.

If I were president of the United States,

I'd spend fifteen hours a day worrying about my re-election

And,

I'd demand to have my favorite childhood pillow re-stuffed and brought to the White House... in a purple Mercedes Benz.

If I were King of America,

with a veto stamp in one hand and a Cat-O-Nine-Tails in the other, I'd build a moat around Washington, DC and the better parts of Virginia and Maryland, and wear chain mail to bed.

If I were King of America,

I'd have 72 wives 33 mistresses and 4 diversely cute guys, just in case.

I'd build a machicolation on my castle parapet and commit defenestration twice a week,

casting Riff-raff and Wrongdoers into my shark-filled Seas.

If I were King of America

Mutton would be made out of fish.

But...

If I were more omnipotent than God,

the human race would understand more clearly the plight of Job.

If I were more omnipotent than God,

All light would be in darkness,

And

This world would end as easily as it would be to say,

"CURTAIN".

# Never Know

**MARJORIE:**

I never know what I'll do. I think I know. I imagine what I'll do. I see myself doing it. But until the moment actually comes…I drove up in front of my house. As I got out of the car I heard my front door slam. I saw a man running out of my house, my cat running out after him. Instantly I attained aerobic maximum heart rate, my mouth opened, "Hey, you let my cat out." Just like in a dream when you feel stuck in molasses. Then an instinct attack. Fight or flight? Fight or flight? Flight. But I didn't run away, I ran after him! "What were you doing in my house, asshole?" What was he doing in my house? Robbing me, peeing on the carpet, rearranging the furniture like the Manson family? I focused on the hulking figure in front of me. He was big—real big. But he was slow—real slow. I was going to catch him. Then what? Would fear win out, would I kick his ass, would he whip out a .357—gun me down? Rape me, dismember me? I didn't know and I didn't care. I was going to catch him. Suddenly he fell flat on the asphalt in front of me. I cursed him as he slowly rose, drawing back his Virginia ham fist. I smelled the beer on his breath, I saw the glaze in his crystal blue eyes. He said nothing, but bathed in the sodium vapor street light I heard every word, "Bitch, I'm drunk, high, fat and exhausted. Please stop chasing me." But I didn't listen. I pursued until he fell and fell again and at last skulked between two houses into the dark. I called the police; picked the guy out of a photo line-up. He was arrested, jailed, tried and convicted all thanks to—Marjorie Fitzsimmons: Crime Stopper. I felt like Christie Love, Pepper Anderson and all three Charlie's Angels rolled into one. You never know what you'll do.

CURTAIN

# Jeffrey, et al.

*[Genevra is sitting on stage with 7 candles, which she begins to light
as soon as she starts speaking.]*

**GENEVRA:**

I seem to continually
find myself in this
position I said.

He remained silent,
smiled
slightly as his leg
inched closer to my...

Instead I confused him
and came home the
next morning to other
arms
     legs
        thighs
           lips
              eyes

then watched them go with
amusement,
befuddlement,
and a slight(ly subverted)
wistfulness.

*[At each asterisk (*) below, she blows out one of the candles.]*

And you ignore me. *
And you are too scared. *
And you are too insecure. *
And you are too dumb. *
    You want a mommy. *
    You want a tart. *

And I just want someone
who doesn't translate into
    fear.

*[She blows out the last candle and is left in darkness.]*

CURTAIN

# He Was Lying, He Was Drunk

*[Greg stands at the lip of the stage. A sheet is stretched over his chest and held by cast members who stand to either side of him. As he delivers the following text, Greg leans further and further into the sheet until he is standing nearly at a 45° angle to the audience. As the sheet takes more and more of his weight it becomes more and more difficult for Greg to speak until he can only do so in a whisper.]*

**GREG:**

The man wore grey, polyester pants and a red shirt opened wide at the chest. The man wore dirty white tennis shoes and a single gold colored chain. The man was singing. He held a cup in his hand, a coffee cup, itself held together in places with tape. There were pictures of playing cards on the cup—an ace of diamonds, a jack of clubs—but they were obscured by the tape and the hand of the man. On his other hand he wore a ring, a single steel band without ornament, and wide. And with this steel band he beat out the rhythm to his song on the bars of the train. He grasped the bars to steady himself as the train entered and exited the stations along the way, and with the same hand he snapped down his ring on the bars. He moved through the car as he sang, and people moved in their seats and where they stood, where they held onto the bars, to avoid him. This was eight-thirty in the morning, the car was full. People were on their way to work, they didn't want to listen to the man. They didn't want to look at the man, but they couldn't avoid doing so. He sang about Jesus. He sang about heaven. He sang about a savior that waited for us all. His eyes were closed and his face was turned to the flourescent lights above, it sparkled with sweat. At that moment there was no escape from the man, he stank up the train. He smelled of garbage and stale beer. Some people recoiled visibly at his approach, they were disgusted and they didn't hide that feeling. His hair was grey and pressed to the side, his teeth were absolutely white. The man sang as loud as he could but it wasn't really very loud. His voice was broken in some way. I imagined that it must have been strong at one time, it sounded like it had been. But now it was broken, and the sound of the ring on the bars pierced his voice with every rap and obscured it. He said love was all that mattered in the world and I congratulated myself on seeing that he was lying.

CURTAIN

# The Age Of Wisdom, The Age Of Foolishness

**SEAN:**

This is my copy of *War and Peace*. It's nice and old and worn. This is my globe. The ocean is brown, not blue. Blue is for high schoolers. Brown is like what smart people have in their dens or libraries. Why are these things in my home? I do not use them. They are there to make me look smart. But they do not do their job. See, truly smart people know that dumb people use these things to make them look smart. I'm smart enough to know that, but too dumb to do anything about it. Actually, I didn't really know this until my girlfriend was in my apartment and saw my copy of *War and Peace*. She said, "You have never read that. You have it here to make you look smart."

See, she is a truly smart person. Or so I thought. I was at her apartment and I noticed that on her bookshelf she, too, had a globe, with a brown ocean. And a copy of *War and Peace*. It was in plain view. Then I looked closer. Not in plain view was this book: *My Own Book of Bible Stories*. And this book: *Sharks!* If I were a truly smart person I might suspect that she was...

We both haven't read *A Tale of Two Cities* either.

CURTAIN

# Doug Sanders is Dead

**SCOTT:**

Doug Sanders is dead, girls, so grab a needle and stitch another square on that goddamn quilt. Doug Sanders is dead and who gives a good goddamn except some queens in Lower Manhattan and his sweet old mother in New Mexico. 30 years old he was, I guess, and dropped like a log, I'm told. Two weeks after he was diagnosed, they say, he was gone. He was always proud of his skinny stick arms and legs, so there wasn't much of him to waste and waste away he did. "What a bitch, huh?" as he would say and laugh his wicked laugh, "heheheheheh."

We were friends in college. In a class of 12 it's that or enemies and I always liked Doug, half Cherokee, shoulder-length blond hair, blue eyes and razor sharp wit and I liked to make him laugh his wicked laugh "heheheheh." What I miss most about him though is his other laugh. The laugh he learned from his mother, the laugh he saved for things that were supposed to be funny but weren't. The parody of polite laughter, the laugh that says "I would laugh now, just to be nice, but I really can't be bothered," shshshshshsh, went that laugh shshshshshsh. But now both those laughs are gone because Doug Sanders is dead.

I lost contact with Doug after he moved to NYC. I heard that he had become "political" and was doing theater in support of ACT-UP. I found this rather shocking behavior for when I knew Doug he was devotedly apolitical, unless the topic at hand was bad acting, personal grooming or canasta.

I'm afraid that Doug would not like this play. Too dull, too earnest, too straight, (in every sense of the word). But there is not a lot that he can do about that now for Doug Sanders is dead and since the dead cannot write, we will never know what kind of play that Doug would have written about his own death.

"The Extremely Sad and Tragic Death of the Simply Fabulous and Positively Dreamy Doug Sanders as told by Doug Sanders starring Doug Sanders and the Doug Sanders Dancers in Sense-Surrounding Fashion-Enhanced Glamour Vision."

"Enter Doug Sanders, his amber hair translucent in the soft moon glow, his taut frame loosely encumbered by a white strapless chiffon gown (only, of course, if the play is to be performed after Memorial Day and before Labor Day for god sakes, otherwise, substitute, ecru for white), on a swing. As our hero begins to sing the street singer's lament that opens *Three Penny Opera*, he is struck dead." Shshshshhshsh.

But Doug Sanders is dead and we will never hear that laugh again.

But they say that the dead will never die as long as they live on in our minds. So for today, Doug Sanders is alive, Miss Thing. He's playing canasta and he's kicking ass. Hehehehehehehe.

CURTAIN

# MetaMania MetaFest 2000

*[Music: "One Note" by Stan Getz & Charlie Byrd. Andy's recorded voice on voice-over. As soon as the play is started, the tape is played and Andy comes out, sits in a chair at a table and writes in his notebook.]*

## ANDY: [V.O.]

Hello, ladies and gentlemen and welcome to what is approximately the 110th play Andy Bayiates has written for *Too Much Light Makes The Baby Go Blind*. Only about a third of these plays have made it into the show, and only about two-thirds of them have even been read by other Neo-Futurists, so this is a special play indeed.

Examine Andy's brow. He appears to be in deep thought. I wonder if he's writing a play right now or just making marks on a page. Funny.

I wonder why he wrote this play? Is he simply sick of memorizing lines? There must be more.

Let's look for that truly self-conscious moment when Andy—

*[Andy looks up. Rest in music. Silence. Andy looks back down as music starts up again.]*

## ANDY: [V.O.]

I think that was it.

You know, a little bit of interesting history: Andy wrote a piece similar to this for his first audition with this company.

Neo-Futurists eat this kind of shit up.

Do any of you find it odd that Andy wrote a play in which, I, the voice, play a central role, and in fact I, meaning me, the voice, am him? I'm standing in my apartment in Hyde Park right now, imagining you in Andersonville watching my balding head and listening to my recorded voice. It's a strange life I lead. I wish I could give you a better picture. I wish I could open up that skull of mine and let you peer in. I'd do that for you, you know, if it were possible.

I want to end this play with a big laugh. But it's so difficult to find a good capper for a piece like this.

*[Music stops suddenly. Andy looks up again.]*

**ANDY:**
If I believed in God, I'd want to be a minister.

[*Andy looks back down. Music begins again.*]

**ANDY: [V.O.]**
I guess that will have to do. Curtain.

# Shaken

© 1995 Greg Allen

*[Greg walks on stage holding a sack of sugar.]*

**GREG:**

I remember seeing this commercial—you know the one. The baby's crying and the phone's ringing and the mother's trying to cook dinner. And the baby's crying and the phone's ringing and the dinner's boiling over. And the baby's crying and the phone's ringing and the dinner's boiling over. And the baby's crying and the mother's trying to answer the phone and the dinner's burning. And the baby's crying and the mother's screaming into the phone and the dinner's splashing all over the kitchen. And with this look of fury in her eyes the mother lunges for the baby and the image freezes!

And then this voice-over says something like—"Stop, before you take it out on your child."

And I remember thinking—"God, how horrible! This woman must be crazy! How could you possibly let it get to you to the point of shaking your own baby to death? This ad must be aimed at those single parents who live in the slums with 36 kids and no education."

And now I have my beautiful red-haired, blue-eyed, cute as a pumpkin, eight month old son named Noah. And I get to play with him every day as I take care of him while my wife works. And he giggled on the bed next to me as I wrote this play. And every day his smile fills my heart with joy. But with equal force his cry just sends knives through my soul. So I feed him, and I hold him, and I change him, and I rock him, and I put him to bed.

*[Greg begins to bounce the sack of sugar back and forth between his hands. This gradually escalates through the following speech.]*

But sometimes these things don't work, and the screaming goes on. And it goes on. And I love him more than anything else in the world and I'm responsible for making him feel better now. And I just can't do it. And he screams.

So I pick him up and I move him around to different rooms and he screams. And I smile and I try to laugh it off and I say, "that's okay" and he screams. And I tell myself, "Greg, you should be able to handle this" and it's 3 a.m. and he screams. And I've got money and education and family support and he screams. And I've been non-violent since I was twelve and he screams. And I want it to stop.

I just want to do anything to stop this pain—that he feels, that I feel, that's clawing its way into my heart and tearing my hair out and he screams. And I've read the stories of the horrible, terrible, awful parents who throw their babies out the window or smother them with a pillow and I know it's unthinkable but I am there and he screams. I am there and I want it to stop now. I want to end the screaming and I want to end the pain and I want to just pick him up and SHAKE THE FUCK OUT OF HIM!

[*After escalating to violently shaking the sack of sugar, Greg freezes.*]

But I don't.

So far.

CURTAIN

# Close Your Eyes and Make A Wish;
# June 9, 1934, 1979, now

*This was originally performed on June 9, 1996. Lusia's mother was present in the audience.*

[*Lusia sits center stage. Lights are up full. A birthday cake (store-bought, decorated with flowers and such) is on a table in front of her. Forty-five candles are on the cake. Throughout the course of the monologue Lusia lights the candles and the lights gradually dim to black.*]

## LUSIA:

My mother lights candles in church. She puts a dollar bill, sometimes a five into the basket in front of the church near the alter and lights a candle for my father, Nicholas Strus, at St. Nicholas Cathedral in the Ukrainian Village, where they were married and their daughters baptized, just steps away from the candle she will light and the prayer she will recite or the conversation she will have. I'm not sure which. I know she closes her eyes.

"The light lets him know all is well. It helps him rest," she says.

My father and mother knew each other for two weeks before they married. "When you know you know." she says. They worked very hard and had three daughters and paid for a house and worked very hard and lived. And my father got sick and the cancer spread and her husband, the truck driver, grew tired and small in their bed in their house on the Northwest side and so, my mother worked very hard and he watched his wife, the cleaning lady, watch her husband grow tired and small in their bed in their home on the Northwest side.

Two years. One hundred pounds. He watched his wife work hard to not grow tired. Seventeen years ago. He went to the hospital where their daughters were born a few blocks away from the church where they were married. She phoned him there on the day before her birthday, seventeen years ago, to tell her husband, "We'll all be there tomorrow morning. I'll bring a cake." And he said, "No. Sleep in. You're tired." And she said, "No." And he said, "Sleep." And she said, "It's my birthday." And he said, "Yes. Sleep." And the next morning, my mother received a phone call and the man or the woman on the other end told her her husband had died. Her husband would no longer grow tired and small in their bed in their home on the Northwest side. And to my recollection, we never lit the candles on that cake for my mother's forty-fifth birthday.

My mother will light a candle in church this Sunday. "The light lets him know all is well. It helps him rest," she says.

And he said, "No. Sleep in. You're tired."

[*By now, all the candles have been lit. Lusia blows out all candles, leaving the stage in darkness.*]

CURTAIN

# Jonesin' for Jesus

[*Steve kneels with hands clasped as if praying. Behind him is a large picture of Jesus himself...the blue-eyed version.*]

**STEVE:**

I was raised Catholic, and for me, the scariest thing they made me do when I was a kid was go to confession. You had to kneel in this little room that was so dark, I was terrified of it. My mother made me go, at least once a month. I always felt that was much too soon between confessions because there was never enough time to build up any really bad sins. And just when that cleansed feeling started to go away, and I was ready to commit some really terrible cardinal, venereal sin or whatever it is, there I was, back in the confessional with nothing really to confess! That's why I always had the same one's, too...I lied to my mother, said some bad words, talked back to my father, so I usually had to make stuff up!..." I stole a tortilla from an old lady while she was getting out of her wheel chair," stuff like that. The whole thing just turned me off to religion in general. I don't appreciate the way they scared me into believing what they wanted me to believe in. I try very hard not to rely on what they taught me but it was so ingrained into my head I can't seem to shake it. So, I've become a hypocrite, probably like many of you, using religion when I need it. I hate that about myself. But on the bright side, I guess I really don't have anything to worry about. They always taught me that no matter what I did or where I went, Jesus would always love me. And hey, that's not such a bad fuckin' deal.

[*A short dance with the large photo of Jesus takes place to Tony Bennett singing "I Can't Believe You're in Love With Me" until they're off stage.*]

CURTAIN

# People Like Me Run This Country

©1997 Sean Benjamin

*[Sean sits in a chair facing upstage, looking into a mirror at himself and the audience.]*

**SEAN:**

She says, "people like you run this country." So I say, people like me grew up in enlisted military housing and in trailer parks with fathers who traveled out of state to find work. And they drank and smoked and swore about their lives. And people like that had people like me. Half of the people like me didn't finish high school and college wasn't even an option. People like me change their own oil and brake pads and work as masons and welders and roughnecks on offshore oil rigs. People like me joined the army to escape only to be with more people like me. People like me grew old and watched and wondered what went wrong and why has it gotten worse and call their children once a month. People like me get laid off every winter because of no work.

But I know what you mean: People like me are straight, white males who have no right to say anything cause we're the oppressor (The Man) and are faulted for our inability to see the plight of others. But people unlike me need to stop thinking people like me run this country. When my dad chain smokes cigarettes and drinks his twelve-pack of Old Milwaukee while sitting outside his trailer, it sure the hell ain't with the president.

I tried a lifetime to escape people like me, but people like you don't like that. Neither do I. It's my blood. My people. You see, you don't know people like me. People like me do not run this country. But maybe, I'm just saying maybe, people like you do.

CURTAIN

# the subversivest play you've never

[*Blackout. A handheld spot shines on Andy revealing he is sitting on a tall stool on top of a tall, black, wooden box. His head is as high as the numbers. Andy stares at the audience for a moment.*]

**ANDY:**

You might be wondering why I'm sitting in this stool...on top of this tall wooden box.

[*Silence.*]

Well, if you are, that's simply too bad. In this play, things are going to happen which you will not expect Exeter Tuesday on a broken phonograph.

[*Sings in one falsetto note:*] "I"

[*Blackout. Lights up a second or two later.*]

**ANDY:**

I was not lunching yesterday with a famous person and she did not turn to me and say, "lovely pudding, may I try some of your ass?"

[*Puts clown nose on.*]

When I was a little boy, my sister ran away and came back married to some guy. One morning I watched him beat her up.

[*Takes clown nose off.*]

Have you ever—[*Makes strange face and very bizarre high pitched noise.*] Outside this theater, after you leave, this play will continue. Although I will no longer perform it. On your way out of the theater you will each be offered a tiny piece of pink paper. [*Demonstrates with a huge piece of newspaper.*] You will study the paper. You will take the paper home with you and you will never throw the paper out. As you struggle to comprehend its meaning, you will all understand that meaning has no place in life I'm not married. This whole process will in turn enrich my life...and give it meaning.

[*Silence.*]

Swallow me.

[*Silence.*]

Curtain.

[*Numbers are called, but no one jumps. Andy stares at the audience. Finally, he picks someone out.*]

You there. What do you want to see next?

[*Whichever number is requested, Andy picks some other number near his head.*]

Thank you for playing.

[*Andy calls the next play and this play ends.*]

[*A bucket is placed outside the theater so that exiting audiences will not be able to miss it at the end of the show. A sign, on pink paper, reads "Get Your Tiny Pieces of Pink Paper Here." In the bucket, however, are hundreds of pebbles.*]

# Roadkill, or A Visitation

© 1999 Anita Loomis

[*Anita jogs at a moderate pace around the entire stage. After a few laps she looks at the audience as if to begin speaking but she does not. After another lap, she begins talking as she runs. Her speed gradually increases until she is running at a breakneck pace, her breathing affecting her ability to speak.*]

**ANITA:**

I can run for 45 minutes.

It took me about ten weeks to work up to that. Ten beautiful, summer weeks.

I ran in Scotland and Maryland, in New York City and Chicago. Through city parks, woodsy trails, castle grounds and twice through Graceland Cemetery before the security guard pulled up next to me in low white cruiser and said, "Sir, ah, excuse me, sir. You can't run in here." I just laughed and waved and kept on running. Who was I going to disturb? The dead?

It's been getting colder out now, especially in the mornings. I've been thinking, maybe with the weather change I won't run anymore. It's not like I need to run. It's not like I'm in a race for anything.

Last Tuesday morning, I went out for one last run. I was cold. And I was irritable. And I was completely alone in the park when I heard the gravel crunching behind me. I looked over my shoulder and there, coming up fast was Matthew Shepard. He looked pale and winded, like he'd been running a good long time, like maybe all night. Which seemed possible if he'd made it all the way to Chicago from his hospital bed in Colorado.

He ran up next to me. "Hey, faggot," I said. "Hey, faggot," he said, and we ran together for a while in friendly silence, breathing hard. I started to warm up and the sweat ran down my head and into my ears and down my neck and I wiped it away. Matthew started to bleed from a gash in his skull and it ran into his ears and down his neck. "Does that blood feel like sweat?" I said. "Yeah," he said, "only it hurts more."

Matthew sped up, so I sped up. My legs were tight. Matthew's legs were turning purple with bruises. "Do those bruises feel like muscle cramps?" I said. "Yeah," he said, "only they hurt more."

He sped up again. He was going like a jack rabbit running from a pack of wild dogs across the Wyoming plains at night. I pushed myself. I pushed myself to keep up with the ghost of a man twelve years younger, three inches shorter and fifteen pounds lighter than me.

My lungs caught fire, burning from the oxygen streaming into them through my open mouth. I saw boiling blood spilling out of Matthew's mouth, leaving a foamy scarlet trail on the cinders. And then Matthew Shepard stumbled. And he didn't get up. I reached down to help him but he waved me away saying, "You go girl! You run. You better run for your life."

[*Anita runs offstage.*]

CURTAIN

# A Brief History of the United States of America

© 1996 Greg Kotis

[*Blackout. A single spot fades up to reveal Greg sitting center stage, facing the audience.*]

**GREG:**

A man wanted to tell his son how things were in the world, so one day he took him to a field where they could talk for awhile. "The things of the world are exactly as they seem," he said. "Exactly. Except us. We are not as we seem." "How are we, then, father, if we are not as we seem?" "Well..." said the man, "we are like a fog. A fog. Each of us, we are like a cloud which floats about from day to day waiting to dissolve, waiting for a single breath to scatter the mist which makes up our bodies." He pointed to a tree. "That tree there is exactly what it is. It is hard. It will live for two hundred years. The birds which perch upon its branches, they too are exactly as they seem. They too are hard. They haven't the slightest idea what will happen to them in five seconds time. But we— you and I—we are different. We are like a fog." "I don't understand," said the boy. "No?" said the man, gathering his thoughts to explain. "A soldier goes to war, a shell bursts beside him. It takes away his arm. His legs. Did the bomb ever burst? No. Were the bones ever real? The blood that he lost? No. They were not. The soldier, you see, was like a fog. And the bomb? A wind which blew (breath) and so carried the fog away with it. But not all of it. Not even most of it. Leaving the soldier incomplete." The father took his son by the hand and they walked home. The boy became a man who had children who he one day wanted to tell how things were in the world. He took them to the same field his father had brought him, but at the moment of truth he faltered. "You see that?" said the boy-now-a-man. "That's a tree. And upon it? Those are birds." And they walked home. The man-once-a-boy was afraid that his children might not believe him. He was sure of it, in fact, and from that time forward avoided their skepticism in all things. Years later, the boy-long-since-turned-man lay on his death bed feeling his body falling apart. But that wasn't quite right, it wasn't falling apart. It was coming apart. Drifting apart and heading up and down and toward each and every point of the compass. And the only thoughts he couldn't keep from his mind were, "I'm so glad he told me. I'm so glad he told me."

CURTAIN

# Pope Jolen

© 1995 Stephanie Shaw

*[Spoken while mixing and applying Jolen cream bleach to upper lip, with help of small mirror if necessary.]*

**STEPHANIE:**

As a kid I had these two favorite sixteenth century Italian noblewomen.

(What young girl doesn't?)

The first, Lucrezia Borgia; whose very name conjured up for me images of Alchemy, Treachery, Dark Poisons. I pictured her a lute-plucking witchy woman out behind the castle having sex after midnight sort of thing; voracious, salty, hairy, bloody, magic soaked. I wanted to be just like her.

Then I got older, and I found out that her fierce reputation was exaggerated. She was actually a very good Catholic. So devout in fact, that she slept with the Pope. Her father. Who subsequently married her off five times. She died at the age of thirty-nine. Not surprisingly.

Well.

I switched my sights to Catherine de' Medici. I decided I was going to pattern my life after hers. So far that's been a washout. By the time she was my age she was married to the King of France, had ten children and was designing chateaux. And while I can't say for certain that she didn't give a shit about the hair on her upper lip, I'm guessing it didn't bother her. She was far too busy fighting the Catholic extremists, distinguishing heresy from sedition and defying the Pope.

The only things we really have in common are that we're both Italian, we both married foreigners and we're both bad Catholics. More than I have in common with Lucrezia, thankfully. Maybe if, like Catherine, I came back with my shield or on it more often, my shield wouldn't say "Jolen".

The problem is, it's so easy to defy the Pope these days.

CURTAIN

# Before You Know It

[*Diana stands center. The text is meant to be spoken as rapidly as sense and comfort will allow, start to finish without pause.*]

**DIANA:**

What are you what are you what are you? Oh my word, oh my, oh my word, my world, my world, my world, you are my world, you are all that is, you are food and move and warm and dry and sound and color, you are all, you are all, you are all different, you are all different from me, you are not part of me, ha! Ha-ha! I am free, l can run and you will chase me, you are a toy, you are my toy, you do what I say almost all the time, ha-ha! You are so neat! What a swell toy, I want to be just like you, I want to be just like you, I want to wear the things you wear, I want to do the things you do be just like you just like you are so weird and just mean and arbitrary in your rules and stuff and why? why? why? what is your problem, I would rather die than be like you are everything I hope I never am, you just wrong wrong way wrong way way wait a minute, one minute, you just you just you are just like we are just like we are very similar, you are pretty cool sometimes, you used to be young and you had sex and read poetry and danced 'til late and drank like a fish and you were like me like me you're like me like you I'm like you're old but you're okay, you are okay, you're okay are you okay, do you feel okay? maybe you should let me get that for you lie down for a while I call the doctor, okay? You're here you go go go going, where are you going where do you go where do you go sometimes I don't know where you've gone, where you go, where'd you go, where'd you where've you gone mom, mom, mom? mom.

CURTAIN

# Promises, Possibilities, and a Disturbing Lack of Ventilation

© 1999 Noelle Krimm

*[Noelle is lying on her back on the floor in the center of the stage. The lights are dim.]*

**NOELLE:**

I lie here on the floor in the twilight of the empty room, hoping for a breeze, and simultaneously cursing myself and thanking you for bringing me here. And for the first time in days or maybe weeks or more, I am completely alone and not the least bit lonely as I lie here safe and just a little too warm in a room filled with nothing…so nothing is out of reach.

CURTAIN

# In Defense of the Fantasy Section

[*Steph enters brandishing a broadsword.*]

**STEPHANIE:**

This is the sword and sorcery section of our show, and if you can't handle that, well, you can kiss my ass.

This is where the pale boys gather and the quiet girls gravitate in the dull hours of the afternoon. They come here to feed their rich imaginary lives with triumph and sex in the form of brawny Caucasian men defending women who faint like lilies while their breasts pop from artfully shredded rags and fire breathing demons threaten.

Here, politics are simple, even if they are not correct. Here, women are currency and men earn them through action. Here, monsters sin monstrously and meet their deserved end. Here, all is primal and prurient and there is nothing more important than killing the dragon and maintaining the status quo—as long as it benefits the good guy and the good guy is us.

This section of the show could almost be a plank in the Republican platform.

What are you doing here?

[*Stephanie begins executing some broadsword work; lights fading to spot.*]

The awkward boys and the silent girls, we come here the way we come to a six pack of Pepsi and a bag of orange circus peanuts. With relief, defiance, glee, even. Here, my god!, we can live a while without wincing. We can meet the enemy and find that it looks nothing like us; that it has skin problems far more bizarre and advanced than any we will ever have to encounter in the mirror. Here we can dream of a magic that can be snatched from the ether and manipulated by the adept, we can force fate to deliver with any sort of topping we desire.

Here, we go ahead and feed the beautiful virgin to the beast, and we laugh and we laugh and we laugh, because we know she's no virgin. We know the bitch has probably had her pick.

Here we can murder with our bare hands and come out smelling like Brut by Fabergé.

[*Lights change.*]

This has been the sword and sorcery portion of our program. And if you didn't like it, well then, you can kiss my ass.

CURTAIN

# Digging Up the Dead

© 2001 Sean Benjamin

*[Blackout. Sean is sitting at a table. He lights a match before he starts speaking and holds it up in front of his face.]*

**SEAN:**

You are the only animals that dig up your dead
To examine bones
For answers to a past
To recreate a history

*[He uses that match to light another one. He drops the old match into an ashtray and lets it continue to burn. He repeats this after each stanza.]*

Inside insignificant findings
You find significance
You can't let go where you are from

Neither can I
I'm the same animal you are
Ask me about my dead

Burned and buried
Deep in Adirondack dirt
No answers will come from there
Not to your questions
Or mine

Dig up my dead
And all you'll find:

I'm descended from ashes

*[He drops the last match into the ashtray and blows them all out.]*

CURTAIN

# Freshmen

© 1997 Greg Allen

**GREG:**

So it's the early 80's.

I've spent my entire life in the cozy sheltered protection of my family's armpit: Wilmette, Illinois.

I go to college.

A small liberal Liberal Arts school in the cow fields of Ohio. And... I ... fall in love with A GAY MAN! A GAY MAN! I FALL IN LOVE WITH A GAY MAN! Well actually I don't really know if he's gay, I mean I don't think he's gay—BUT OF COURSE I'VE NEVER MET ANYONE WHO'S GAY. WHAT'S GAY? WHO'S GAY? WHAT THE FUCK IS GAY? HE'S GOT HIS HAND ON MY DICK BUT IS THAT GAY? DOES THAT MEAN HE'S GAY? DOES THAT MEAN I'M GAY? I MEAN I'M **NOT** GAY! I MEAN I DON'T FEEL GAY! I MEAN I'VE NEVER BEEN GAY! And he's never been gay, as far as I know—BUT MAYBE HE **IS** GAY! HE'S GOT HIS HAND ON MY DICK SO HE MUST BE GAY! BUT I'VE GOT MY HAND ON HIS DICK AND IT'S THIS WEIRD LITTLE KNOBBY THING WITH A LITTLE BEND IN IT! IT'S GOT THIS LITTLE BEND IN IT LIKE A LITTLE BOOMERANG OR SOMETHING, AND I DON'T KNOW WHAT TO DO WITH IT! I MEAN I'VE NEVER SEEN AN ERECT PENIS! I MEAN OF COURSE I'VE SEEN MY OWN ERECT PENIS BUT I'VE NEVER SEEN **SOMEONE ELSE'S**! MUCH LESS **"TOYED"** WITH IT! AND I DON'T KNOW WHAT TO DO! I DON'T KNOW WHAT TO DO! I DON'T KNOW WHAT TO DO! I DON'T KNOW WHAT TO DO! AND HE SUCKS ME OFF AND I JERK HIM OFF AND HE SUCKS ME OFF AGAIN AND I AM FLIPPING OUT! I AM FREAKING OUT! I AM FUCKING FLIPPING FREAKING OUT! AND I'M RUNNING AROUND THE ROOM GOING WAAAAAAHHHHHH!!!!! INSIDE MY HEAD I'M RUNNING AROUND THE ROOM GOING WAAAAAAAHHHHHHH!!!!!!!! AND SO FINALLY FINALLY FINALLY FINALLY FINALLY FINALLY FINALLY FINALLY FINALLY I AVOID HIM AND I FIND A GIRLFRIEND AND I FUCK HER.

And she knows him.

They went to highschool together.

Her roommate is his best friend.

And we'd all been hanging out together all semester.

And he was the most brilliant, inspiring, affectionate, influential person in my life.

And we don't really talk again for over three years.

And when we finally do talk it's not the same.

And I live to regret it the rest of my life.

But I was young,

And inexperienced,

And confused.

And I didn't realize until years later that I was in love with him.

And I've never really loved another man before or since.

And now I'm happily married and have two wonderful kids.

And if I had it to do over again...

I would take that dick and suck him dry.

CURTAIN

# Fascism: A Picturebook For Children

[*Anita is seated in a chair. She opens a large blank book out toward the audience and "reads" from it upside down, turning the always-blank pages as if to show illustrations.*]

**ANITA:**

Once upon a time, a long long time ago, in a land far far away from here, something happened that was very bad. It was very very very bad. The people who did this thing were very very very very bad people. The something that happened a long long time ago in a land far far away from here was so bad that it cannot be described in this story because nothing even remotely this bad happens today anywhere near here or anywhere at all. This very very very very bad something that happened could not even possibly happen today because there are no longer any bad people like the bad people who did this very very very very bad thing. There are no pictures of this very very very very bad something that can be shown. If pictures of this very very very bad something and these very very very bad people were to be shown, then this very very very bad something and these very very very bad people might upset the very very good people of today and then something very very very very bad might happen. But thankfully, this is not once upon a time, a long long time ago in a land far far away, so something very very very bad can never happen here. The End.

[*The book is closed.*]

CURTAIN

# Democracy InAction

*[Connor enters and addresses the audience.]*

**CONNOR:**
Raise your hand if you'd like this play to be over now.

*[The raised hands of the audience are counted and if they represent a majority, "Curtain" is called. If not, Connor asks the audience a question about current political events. After facilitating discussion for a few moments, Connor repeats his first line and tallies the votes. This cycle repeats until a majority of the audience votes to end the play.*

*A note on the content of this play: Rather than just a current events "quiz," this play attempts to encourage a real (if brief) discussion about our political system. Questions about current legislation, matters of domestic and foreign policy, and the structure of our representative democracy should be stressed. The personal lives of politicians as well as any scandals not directly related to the legal governing of our nation should be avoided. If the answers from the audience tend to be partisan, try to solicit opposing or differing views. Ignore, cut short or, as a last resort, mock any member of the audience who tries to use this play to capitalize on being the center of attention.]*

# Night of the Living Hypochondriac

[*Rachel in a chair with a blank sheet of paper. Tight spotlight on her. The rest of the cast supply the Voices, which overlap, whispering very quietly, from all over the room, throughout her monologue.*]

**VOICES:**
His soul swooned slowly as he heard the snow falling faintly through the universe and faintly falling, like the descent of their last end, upon all the living and the dead.

**RACHEL:**
Whenever I feel a case of writer's block coming on, I have the same daydream. I'm sleeping and I wake up and James Joyce is standing over me with a big knife. He holds onto my arm with his big dry hand and slashes my wrist [*she tears paper in half*] and all these words come pouring out. Or he whacks me so hard on the back of the head that it shatters all my teeth [*she crumples half the paper, drops it*] and sentences start leaking out my nose. He looks at me very hard and I realize I can see right through his body. [*She slowly rips rest of paper into tiny pieces.*] I look right through his body and I see layers and layers of thin transparent ghosts sifting through the room, piling up in drifts, all their words clinging to them like old grey moss, shifting gently to settle all around me, falling faintly through the universe and faintly falling, all around me, falling, like snow.

[*Voices should slowly drop out one by one. Rachel lets the rest of the paper pieces flutter to the floor. Curtain is called when last voice drops out.*]

CURTAIN

# Clean House

[*Phil is cleaning up the theater.*]

**PHIL:**

I like a clean house.

I like order.

There's a place for everything and everything in its place.

Beth works long hours so I try to take care of the dishes and laundry and stuff when I can.

Plus we have a guest now.

My friend, Chet, is staying at our place.

He's keeping his stuff at our place.

Until he moves.

To L.A.

He's an actor, too.

He's going through a divorce right now, so he's been moving around a lot, staying here and there.

I was kind of surprised when he told me that they were separating.

Kinda. Not too much.

I was a witness at their wedding.

I wish I'da known he was considering this. Then I could've...

I dunno.

[*He's finished cleaning.*]

There.

CURTAIN

# A Very, Very Neo-Futurist Play

© 2000 Noelle Krimm

*[Noelle enters with suitcase and begins speaking as soon as "Go" is called. She sits down on the lip of the stage, opens the suitcase, and removes her boots. All of the actions are performed concurrently with the text.]*

**NOELLE:**

This is a very, very Neo-Futurist play. I say that because it encompasses more components of the Neo-Futurist aesthetic than any play I have written in the past. First of all, I am just being myself, speaking to you. That's a biggie in Neo-Futurism because we don't play characters, we don't try to suspend your disbelief, there's no fourth wall. In fact, that's what I should be doing in every play I perform on this stage. I should be myself and be truthful. The problem is *[Noelle reaches into the suitcase and retrieves a box of make-up remover towelettes and removes her make-up.]* the actual everyday me doesn't wear make-up and even if I do, I don't wear nearly this much. But I always wear it in the show because it makes me feel more confident.

Also, in the show I tend to wear shirts that I feel are especially flattering for whatever reason *[Noelle stands, removes her shirt, retrieves a large sweatshirt from the suitcase and puts it on.]* whereas during the week, I tend to wear big sweaters and sweatshirts. And, in the show, I tend to wear pants that I feel make my ass look nice. *[Noelle removes an old pair of baggy jeans and a pair of briefs from suitcase and puts them on the floor.]* And in attempting to make my ass look its best, I wear a thong. Now, I don't wear a thong every day. It feels funny. But I always wear one in the show because it makes me feel more confident. *[Noelle pulls two women from front row up onto stage.]* Audience participation — another biggie in Neo-Futurism. *[Noelle removes a large beach towel from the suitcase and hands one end to each woman. She positions the women as far upstage as possible for obvious reasons, and stands behind the towel which covers her from just below her breasts to just above her knees. Noelle then removes her pants and thong, picks up her jeans and briefs and puts them on during the following chunk of monologue.]* Of course, if I were going a hundred percent Neo-Futurist, I would just drop my pants right in front of you but I took off my make-up earlier and I'm feeling less confident. No, actually, even if I was wearing make-up, I would not be dropping my pants in front of you. Not that I think I look bad because I really don't. *[Noelle addresses the women holding the towel.]* You two can feel free to confirm. *[The women would sometimes confirm but would more often giggle and turn red. Noelle would respond however she deemed appropriate at the time.*] You know, there's this guy over at Simon's [*a nearby bar*] named Pete whom I've met, like, thirty times because he's always so drunk he never remembers me. And every time I walk away from whatever conversation we're all having, he turns to Sean and says "She's got a nice ass." And Sean says "My girlfriend?" and Pete says "Oh. Sorry, man." And then later on, Sean tells me about it and it makes me feel good about myself. Isn't that ridiculous? Thank you, ladies. I appreciate it. [*Noelle takes the towel from the women and sends them back to their seats. She then sits down on the lip and puts on a pair of old sneakers.*]

I have a little confidence problem. But doing theater was always OK because I could be someone else, look like someone else, and say someone else's words. It was easy. But becoming a Neo-Futurist meant breaking down all those barriers between myself and the audience and I've realized that to compensate, I've been "Me" but a slightly more polished version of "Me" [*Noelle takes out her contacts and puts them in the suitcase and takes her glasses from suitcase and puts them on.*] with make-up and "nice ass pants" and contacts instead of my glasses and I tend to write a lot of funny plays because when you laugh at something I wrote, I get a little boost.

As far as this being a very Neo-Futurist play, Rachel (one of the other Neo-Futurists) recently made the comment that she felt it was about time I wrote a play that scared the shit out of me. That's very Neo-Futurist, you know. We challenge ourselves. And I couldn't think of anything that would really scare the on-stage persona of me. But *ME* me (even though you may not see a huge difference between the two) is, at the very least, really uncomfortable right now and probably will be for the rest of the show. And that is what makes this a very, very Neo-Futurist play.

CURTAIN

# Ghost Cycle

[*Stephanie sits center with a glass of ice water.*]

**STEPHANIE:**
She was not tall. I was short. Shorter than I am now.

I was a chick, a child, a cherub, a kid, a lass, a lamb. She liked us little ones, and we, the neighborhood kids, we liked her. She talked to us like we were real grown up people. (She was cool.)

That summer night when the block party was winding down to the amplified, distorted strains of Tony Orlando and Dawn, she pointed her finger at me and smiled. I accepted her invitation and we went for a walk, she in her Dr. Scholl's, I on my Big Wheel.

Together, we toured the quieter areas of our quiet suburb. I don't remember what we said. Or even if we said anything. All I remember is the rhythm of my Big Wheel...and the clinking of the ice in her glass of Scotch. [*Stephanie rattles the ice in her glass for a long moment.*] A very adult sound.

That night, perhaps hours after our walk, she went into her garage, taking with her dreams of the children she had never had, could never have; started the car, and went on a vacation without opening the garage door.

I don't remember her name. But I do remember the wall in her living room, covered with photographs of babies, babies, none of them hers— nieces, nephews, cousins, friends. Babies that did not belong to her.

And contemplating, now, my own mantelpiece which is becoming crowded with photographs of babies, babies, none of them mine, nieces and nephews, all of them dear, I wonder. Why did she choose me? What was it that she recognized in me? Why did she take me on that walk? And every twenty eight days or so, when, in spite of all our efforts, the cramps hit (reminding me of ice expanding in a glass of Scotch) I continue to wonder...why is she still taking me on that walk?

CURTAIN

# An Athletic Play With Bad Language

© 1997 H.A. Riordan

[*HEATHER is pedaling furiously on a bike on some sort of immobilizing device, like a wind trainer.*]

**HEATHER:**
Move mothafuckamothafuckamothafucka
Move mothafuckamothafucka
Move.

Get out get out get out of my way
get out get out get out.

Don't
Don't park there.
You can't park there.
Illegal! Illegal Parker! Burn in Hell! Die a thousand deaths!
Die die die die die

OK OK OK let's go let's move let's move
green light

Greeeeen light!!

make it make it make it make it
made it made it made it

OK OK OK OK
How do those guys ride those tiny kids' bikes with their knees up at their chins?
Jesus.

OK, OK, OK move move.

Hey asshole, if you can't use your turn signal, why don't you snap it off the driving column and shove it up your ass?

OK OK OK, let's move let's
Move mothafuckamothafuckamothafucka
Move mothafuckamothafucka
Move.

CURTAIN

# My Play's on Time

© 1998 Lusia Strus

[*Lusia sits in a chair. A bright interrogation light goes on and ticking clock sound is heard. Text in upper case is either amplified or, if possible, a voice-over.*]

**LUSIA:**

THE TIMER HAS BEEN SET.

And my play—My play is

IS NOT A DRESS REHEARSAL.

Is passing. Right now. Right now this play
is passing. This day. This
hour. This—No
This—No This—No This Second

IS THE REAL THING

Is passing. Two minutes. 120 seconds. It's the time I have.
All the time I -
Only the time I—
The time I have to

SPEND TIME WISELY

To use. To fill. To...Oh my God. To waste. I'm wasting time. I have to
make this time count. I need to say something devastatingly important.
Something. Something.
Something funny. Say something. Do. Do. Do something.
Something perfect.
Because

TIME IS RUNNING OUT

And this has to be the best play in the *whole*

HALF TIME!

[*Lights up full. Lusia gets out of the chair and leads the cheer:*]

You can do it!
If you set your mind to it!
So buckle down! Buckle down!
Do it! Do it! Do it!

[*Return to interrogation light. Ticking resumes. Lusia sits back down.*]

Okay. I'm back. And I can use this time to my fullest advantage. I can say something necessary. I can. I can. I can do my play—

Is passing.

My play is passing. Right. Right.

Right now. No now. No now. No now. No. Now.

[*Ticking stops.*]

TIME'S UP.

[*Blackout.*]

CURTAIN

# Sometimes I Get a Wee Bit Cranky
# When My Blood Sugar Drops Too Low

© 2000 H.A. Riordan

**VOICES:**

waiting for the bus waiting for the bus waiting for the bus the bus never came [*Repeats, sotto voce.*]

**HEATHER:**

I'm standing, waiting for the bus, waiting for the bus. A bus that will not arrive. The people who wait for the bus, myself excluded, look like they've been waiting for the bus forever. The bus stop is by the hospital. Like the hospital, the bus stop is depressing. I can hardly wait for the bus there. Besides, the bus will never arrive. There is even a sign for a bus route that no longer, or ever, existed. Or maybe it does; but I don't know anyone who's ever taken that bus.

The thing is, I don't want to be waiting for this bus. I would rather be biking or driving, or not traveling so far west, or see the bus from a half a block away, and triumphantly run to the entrance, just before it pulls off. If this bus ever comes, it will meander, I can just tell.

The old woman next to me, waiting for the bus that will not arrive, is crazy, or sick, or both. She is saying "cancer, cancer, cancer," over and over and over. I don't know if she is newly diagnosed, or just wants everyone to be aware of her zodiac sign. I just want her to shut up. She's giving me that crazy look that says "I'm crazy so I can blather on and talk however loud I want." I want an aspirin for this headache that she's given me that's a mile long, or her head on a platter, either with or without the aforementioned cancer. I have no sympathy for the cancer woman, in fact, I've decided it's because of her that the bus isn't coming. I've decided that she is trying to give me cancer. If this tumor that I have recently discovered turns out to be cancer, I will be forced to hunt her down and kill her, for giving me this cancer. I decide if she says cancer one more time I will pull out my ovaries and throw them at her. She is purposely ruining my day. Or my life. I can't be sure which.

Instead I walk to the next stop, which is deserted, because, of course, the bus will never arrive, and it's only the crazies that hang out at the previous bus stop that give the impression that there's actually any bus service in this part of town. It feels good to wait alone, even if the bus never comes.

CURTAIN

# SURFER OF THE NIGHT

[*Rob sits on stage in chair with a remote. Blue TV glow lighting.*]

**ROB:**

I've had this dream before—
I have had this dream:

I am there
    my hair is longer—bleached out,
    I'm sittin' in my
    strato-lounger,
    aqua blue strato-lounger,
    riding
    riding out a killer cable wave,
    late night caught like many nights before.
When the cheeky chair in which I sit,
    chides me with, "Hey surfer boy
    Get up you lazy heavy bastard
    'cause you're pissing me off!"
"Uh, shut up!," I say, "and take it like the chair you are!"
as I flip the foot rest up and kick back.

With a cry of a gull and a "Surf's Up!" from the clouds
The remote appears in my hand;
I catch a power surge and hang ten
    toward a conscious numbing tube ride.
I watch with my eagle eyes, slide in easy,
    recline and surf—

    E!
    E!
    E!
    A & E
    A M C
    T N T
    N B C
    T M C
    A B C
    B E T
    HISTORY
    C N N
    E S P N
    E S P N 2

V  H  1
M  T  V
Flow Bee
Flow Bee
Flow Bee

The Flow Bee?
Pulled unexpectedly into a Flow Bee info-mercial,
   the power of the hoover haircut
   vacuum your hair into style
   the dustbuster do

I scan for a lifeguard, call on the remote power;
   looking to bail, Baby, bail,
   but I careen into a Dead Battery Wipe Out—
    batteries spent
   Must . . . Have . . . New . . .Bat..ter..ies
    Stuck in the suck and ebb of the Flow Bee current
     twirling spinning hanging onto the lounger for life

When a box with 'Box Full of Batteries'
   written on it buoys before me.

   saved
   change batteries saved
   escape the drowning sound of Flow Bee saved

I cling to the lounger
   raise the remote high above my body weak, shaking, wet
      to change
      to switch
      to vanquish the Killer Bee . . .

And in come these dancing eggplants
 in matching striped shorts
 singing and dancing
 "The Dancing Eggplant Song"

   'Weeee are the
   Dancing Eggplants
   Bulbous — Purple
   Dancing Eggplants
   Love us — Watch us

Dancing Eggplants
We love you, so
drink your juice.'

And with that they dance off;
Leaving me to flounder hanging on to the lounger
   the Battery Box now spewing dead batteries
   the T.V. spewing "No more expensive 30 dollar haircuts!"
   & the remote spewing . . . nothing . . . no power . . .
           dead in the water . . .
           dead in the night
           info images stinging my eyes
           burning into my mind

and as I sink
    deeper
    and deeper
    into an aural insanity,
    a visual mediocrity,
    a mind melting victim of late night paid programming
        programming ramming and beating, and beating and ripping,
        and burning and beating and
        beat beat beat beat

this Fuzzy Pink Drum Slammin' Bunny snags my hand
and drags me to safety
    pulls me from . . . strange . . .
    lets me go . . . strange . . .
    my head fells so . . . strange . . .

I'm in a library.
I'm in a Public Library.  No Bunny.
I'm in a Public Library, no Bunny, no TV,
I'm in a Public Library, no Bunny, no TV,
   surrounded by several oversized romance novels,
      that all
      MONKEY PILE!
         on ME!

And this is odd, here
I'm below,
  being crushed—
  books above—
  and while on top
  they all introduce themselves,
  like we're at some Hollywood party.

    'Hi, I'm Waller's The Bridges of Madison County.'
    'Hi, I'm Bronte's Wuthering Heights.'
    'Hi, I'm Tolstoy's Anna Karenina.'
    'Greetings, I'm Roget's Thesaurus.'

Hi, I, Hi.
Truly
I've had this
I have had this
  this same, exact, precise dream
  previously, before, in the past,
  and I am
    I am
    I am Scooby Doo Scared!

CURTAIN

# Lite

*[The following is performed in a dramatic spotlight.]*

**PHIL:**

I laid in bed the other night and watched the light hit your face.

The room was dark. The sun hadn't yet come up.

But the shade was open a bit and the street light shone in and lit up your face.

And I gazed. As if for the first time.

When was the last time I watched you for this long?

How many times have I missed the light falling across your face?

The way a sunset brushes your hair,

candles blink in your eyes,

a campfire kisses your cheeks.

I must have watched your sleeping face for hours.

And as the morning light crept in to wake you, I thought to myself,

"I am gonna be so fucking tired tomorrow."

CURTAIN

# Got Buddha?

[*Steve sits in a chair center with a stuffed animal in his hands. Periodically, as is appropriate with the text, he drops the animal, stares at it, picks it up again. Andy stands behind the chair, reading from a large book.*]

**ANDY:**

A man finds himself communicating. There is a listener, and a speaker. The listener rarely listens. Nevertheless, the speaker continues to communicate.

A baby throws his stuffed dog onto the floor from his high chair. His mother picks it up and gives it back to him. Again, the baby throws his stuffed dog from the high chair. Again, his mother picks it up.

Eventually, mother grows weary of picking up baby's stuffed dog. She stops. Baby has not understood that Freudian business of separating self from other yet. So don't get it into your heads that this is a story about a boy who grows up resenting his mother over a stuffed dog. No. Baby still thinks mother is a part of himself at this point. Baby still thinks the universe bends to his wishes.

So baby instead, cannot understand why life is screwing him.

Baby grows, understands the difference between self and other, and then learns to blame everything on his mother.

Baby goes to high school, scores perfectly on his SAT's, barely experiments with drugs, attends Boston University and majors in Computer Engineering. Baby gets married straight out of college, earns six figures, has a kid, gets a house.

He's only in his early 20's.

Baby's constant reaching, though much like the speaker's constant communicating, consumes him. First job, then wife, then house, then offspring.

And when Baby's life falls apart in his late twenties, when his stuffed dog plummets yet again from his high chair, it is still impossible for Baby to see that the universe is not fucking him.

Speaker has made many attempts to lift Baby from depression because the speaker must communicate what he's learned.

And Baby possesses an incredible mind and listens but cannot learn.

"Perhaps," says the speaker, "it is like when I put a serious, wordy piece into *Too Much Light*. The audience often wanders. I could blame them or I could blame me. Or most important, I could choose not to blame anyone, and I could say to myself 'though the stuffed dog shall fall, I shall learn to stop wanting the dog.' "

CURTAIN

# A Plagiarized Prayer
# For An Enemy Of Thieves

© 1999 Steven Mosqueda

[*Steve rides his bike onto the stage and dismounts, militarily. He holds the bicycle up in front of him, presenting it to everyone. He speaks loudly, reciting a sacred military prayer.*]

**STEVE:**
This is my bicycle. There are many like it but this one is mine. My bicycle is my best friend. It has been so for 11 years. I have mastered it as I have attempted to master my life. Without me my bicycle is useless. Without my bicycle, I am useless. I was without my bicycle for two weeks when it was stolen right in front of my building. Then I saw him. Riding it. In front of my building. Monday. That bicycle is mine, I told him. There are many like it but that one is mine. The enemy replied he had bought it for 50 bucks from another enemy who claimed he had just found it somewhere. The enemy gave my bicycle up freely without confrontation. They are scumbags. They are dreck. They make me want to rip open their chests and shit in their lungs. Before God I swear this creed. My bicycle and myself are symbols of justice. We will strive to be the masters of our enemy. We will be the saviors of what is just and right. So be it. Until there is no enemy, but peace. Amen. [*Under his breath but loud enough to hear:*] ...Fuckers.

CURTAIN

# Corrections and Clarifications

*[Play starts with Scott sitting in a chair at a table reading a series of corrections off 3x5 cards. He has a pencil. Each paragraph below has been written out on a 3x5 card.]*

**SCOTT:**

Due to a printing error, the word "fuckwad" inadvertently appeared in a play performed last week.

Last week we claimed to perform "30 plays in 60 minutes." The correct figure for last week's performance was "28.6 plays in 60 minutes."

In late editions of this show, people may have noticed David Kodeski laughing during his performance of "Not Getting The Joke." This was caused by Lusia Strus moving her tongue and making a funny noise when David Kodeski did not expect her to do so.

When I broke up with Susan Priest in 1986, I told her that it wasn't because I wished to go out with someone else. However, I was lying. I broke up with her so I could go out with Laura Parsons.

In the Sunday edition of this show, people may have noticed Lusia Strus laughing during her performance of "Le Temp." This was caused by David Kodeski moving his body and making a funny noise when Lusia Strus did not expect him to do so.

When I say, "How are you," I mean, "Hello." When I say, "Hello?", I mean, "What do you mean?" When I say, "What do you mean?", I mean, "You're an idiot."

During this edition of this show, people may notice Lusia Strus or David Kodeski laughing during their performances. This will probably be caused by Lusia Strus or David Kodeski moving something and making a funny noise when Lusia Strus or David Kodeski did not expect them to do so.

The Neo-Futurists regret these errors. Fuckwad.

*[Scott grimaces and crosses out the word "fuckwad" thus ensuring that the first "correction" in the play will always be true.]*

CURTAIN

*[NOTE: While this play makes specific references to performers in the show at the time that it was written, you should insert appropriate references to actual performers in your show. For example, always update the "X plays in Y minutes" statistic to reflect your actual experience. The performer should replace the "Susan Priest-Laura Parsons" story with a similar incident of untruthfulness in their life.]*

# N.O.La.

[*We hear a really good brass band music playing underneath. Steve holds an obituary from a newspaper.*]

**STEVE:**

Nowell Joseph "Papa" Glass. Someone you've probably never heard of...he's playing bass drum on this CD. Papa was a drummer with Olympia, one of New Orleans' most popular traditional brass bands. The original Olympia brass band formed in 1883. It was my first jazz funeral. The friends I was visiting read the announcement in the newspaper about Papa's funeral and suggested we go. As we got out of the car my hangover reminded me it was a very hot day, even with the cloud cover. The large crowd lined up and down both sides of Ursulines. Olympia lined up just outside the entrance to St. James, two single file lines. Dressed in suits and ties they quietly tuned their recently shined horns and wiped the beads of sweat and tears from their faces. They waited patiently with the rest of us...the rest of us...a delicious jambalaya of race and color and hair styles and dress, simmering in the humidity together. I've never seen the ingredients for that recipe here in Chicago. And that made me wish...I hate wishing. When Papa was finally brought out, Olympia blew loud and strolled down the street, followed by the long procession of the hearse, limousine, and the rest of us. We followed for a while and then tailed off, returning home to the cool central air and ice cold daiquiris. As I sipped and read Papa's obituary, my hangover slowly dissipated and I began to get hungry...hungry for some more of that jambalaya, waiting for us outside.

[*Steve posts the newspaper clipping on the back wall, upstage.*]

CURTAIN

# The Aluminum Comedian

*[John walks on stage wearing a suit jacket, black dress shoes, and a fedora hat, all of which are too large. He is holding a shot glass filled with water in one hand and in the other hand a pocket watch with its chain bundled up. As he begins the monologue he unrolls a cloth towel, sets it on the floor and stands on it.]*

**JOHN:**

Under the pressure of creation I sunk into myself and found nothing but remnants of my father. These clothes and articles belong to him. This watch. *[He drops the watch, it hangs freely from the chain clasped between his fingers.]* These shoes, 1½ sizes too big for my footsteps. This shot glass, usually filled with some sort of cheap whiskey. And finally, this hat which has visited many doorsteps throughout the greater Chicago area. You see, my father was an aluminum siding salesman. He sold beautiful futures without peeling paint. But what I think he really wanted to be was a stand-up comedian. And that's why I don't think he would mind me finding humor in the fact that his ashes were dumped out of a helicopter over the hills of Montreal. Nor would he be upset with me wearing his clothes or telling one of his jokes, which is what I'm about to do right now. But be warned, I am no joke teller. So please, if you can, picture a man slightly larger than me with gray hair and yellowing skin, picture him sitting in a bar, let's say a Moose Lodge on the corner of Kensington and Rand, on the third stool from the right, but no bar in particular. Picture this man, surrounded by all of his closest friends on that particular afternoon. Picture him telling this joke.

*[John removes his hat with the hand holding the chain, he has no where to put the hat, so he lifts up his leg and places the hat on his foot. He stands on one foot for the rest of the play.]*

"Did I ever show you guys my imitation of a man with a drinking problem?" "No George." "You're the greatest George." "Go ahead, George." *[John makes a toast to the audience.]* "To all. A long and happy life." *[He motions to drink the shot. He misses his mouth and presses it against his forehead. He holds it there. It drips down his face.]* Of course, my father had style, a certain panache I could never in a million years explain in words or costumes or even in my own actions. *[Removes the glass from his forehead. It spills down his face.]*

CURTAIN

# Jimmy, Roger & John

© 1995 Dave Awl

[*In* Too Much Light *the lighting for this piece was accomplished by means of three helpers holding flashlights. However, similar shadow images can be created by other means, and if necessary the text can be performed without special lighting. In the standard staging, the flashlight holders are seated at the edge of the stage in the following locations: Phil downstage center, Anita downstage right, Stephanie downstage left. When Phil's flashlight is on, it casts a large shadow of Dave that looms on the backstage wall. On alternating passages, Phil's flashlight is switched off and Anita's and Stephanie's are switched on, to cast a double shadow on the back wall.*]

[*Play begins in blackout. Dave stands stage center with back to audience. At go, Phil's light snaps on to reveal Dave dancing club style, arms raised over his head, with shadow towering on the back wall. Phil gradually moves the flashlight toward Dave as he speaks to make the shadow loom even larger.*]

**DAVE:**

Seven years ago when you came to the city as a green gay kid with wide eyes and empty pockets, you saw the golden boys [*Phil's light snaps off, Anita & Steph's snap on to create double shadow.*] dancing in the clubs, sweaty and ecstatic, like faerie kings at the height of their glamour with smooth muscles, puppy dog eyes and promising artistic careers. [*Dave slowly lowers his arms, stops dancing, and gradually turns to face audience as he speaks the next passage.*]

You saw their names on posters on lampposts, you saw their paintings in cafes and their drawings on T-shirts in stores and they left you five dollar tips on five dollar checks when they had coffee at the restaurant where you worked. [*Anita and Steph off, Phil back on for single shadow.*] Five years later you saw some of them walking with canes, observed from bus windows making slow deliberate steps across crosswalks on cold winter afternoons, or sitting in cafes with friends to help them stand and sit, like old men at 28, seeming alternately courageous and confused. [*Phil off, Anita and Steph on for double shadow.*]

Some of the people you know who are dying young are artists. Some of them are artists like Shelley and Rimbaud, who produced their greatest work before their mid-twenties. They will be remembered. Some of the people you know who are dying young are artists like Walt Whitman or René Rilke, who produced their greatest work in their later years. They will not be remembered because their train got derailed before it pulled into the station.

[*Anita and Steph off, Phil on for single shadow. Throughout the next few sentences, the stage lights very gradually fade up.*]

And then one night in a darkened movie house you see a trailer for a movie in which Dustin Hoffman chases a diseased monkey around wearing a yellow plastic suit and you are mildly startled to remember that there are people in the world for whom the idea of a plague is still a good subject for entertainment. You wonder if *Longtime Companion* would have done better at the box office if only it had had a few more children and animals in it. [*Stage lights are up full by this point.*] You go home alone. You call one of your friends who's still alive and you don't talk about the past. You talk about the future.

CURTAIN

# SMOOTH

**STEVE:**

When I was around 11 years old, my uncle took me, my brother and sister and my grandmother, his mother, to our first gay pride parade in Los Angeles. It was 1974, right after he first came out. He chose me and my brother to tell first. It went right over my head. I didn't really know what it meant, and it didn't matter anyway. It didn't change the way I felt about him. He was the craziest person in the family which ultimately made him the sanest. I loved him. But I remember as we drove home from the parade that day, in one of my uncle's long line of used, run down cars (upholstery torn, muffler dragging on the road, chipping paint, all of which seemed to bother everyone except my uncle, he loved his cars), I sat in the back seat and looked out the window. I thought to myself, I wonder if I'm gay. I wonder if I'm attracted to other men. I had those thoughts every once in a while after that, and then they just went away. I didn't ask myself that question anymore. I realized I wasn't gay. That part of my life happened pretty smoothly. After my Uncle died, I thought of all the shit he went through with that part of his life, my relatives shunning him, the jokes, the confusion, and I wished it would have been smooth for him, too. He died last year. He was an award-winning teacher and constantly pushed his mostly minority students to settle for nothing but the best. Some of them showed up at his memorial, now college students, some entering med school. I realized how lucky I was to know him and then, to my surprise, I felt glad—I was glad it wasn't smooth for him like it was for me, because then he wouldn't have been who he was—Uncle Leonard.

CURTAIN

# Full Frontal

[*Rachel sitting onstage in a romantic, diffuse backlight with her shirt off and her arms wrapped around her chest. Any reaction from the audience (comments, gasps, whistles, etc.) will lead into the monologue thusly:*]

**RACHEL:**
Oh, no, no no no, this is not what you're thinking.

This is not going to be a sexy play. The light's like this because this is the kind of lighting I would like to be seen in at all times, if that were humanly possible. And my arms are crossed not because I'm trying to be coy, but because frankly, if I uncrossed them, it would be an ugly sight.

See, I have my grandmother's breasts. I have a 25-year-old body and 85-year-old breasts. They are not attractive. They are pale and large and they droop and have stretch marks. I hate them. I have always hated them. Like I hate my thighs, my ass, my hair.

I'm not fishing for compliments. I know how ridiculous it sounds. I didn't write this to turn you on, or off. I guess it's a dedication. To all those girls who look in the mirror and sort of enjoy what they see, except for…this, and except for…that, and those, and the next thing you know those parts represent the whole and you hate yourself. You know what I'm talking about. I'm one of you. I started out strong and grubby and sweaty and chubby and liked it until something went weird and wrong and now I'm sitting here condemning a perfectly decent skeleton and skin, not wanting someone else's body, just the one I used to have before I told myself it was a bad place to be.

All I can say is that people are going to tell you that you're beautiful. Someone will kiss the places you try to conceal, look at you naked and whole and unapologetic. Or they will see you smile, or see you cry, and love you for that. They will not give a good goddamn about your thighs or your nose or your breasts. And they will say look at you, you're beautiful.

Try to believe them. Just try.

CURTAIN

# The New Seekers of The Real Thing

© 1996 Sean Benjamin

[*Sean holds a can of Coke.*]

**SEAN:**

I'm sure this can reminds you of many commercials and many snappy tunes, but what is the song you remember the most when you see this can of Coke?

[*He waits for audience response.*]

"I'd Like to Teach the World to Sing." That's exactly right. Now, do you realize that is actually a real song? It was not written for or by the Coke people. Do you know the real words? Here's the song right now... [*Music begins.*] Do you know who sings it? Do you? [*If no response:* I'll give you a hint. It's in the title of this play. Look at your programs. [*He takes a program from audience member.*] The New Seekers. THE NEW SEEKERS.

I'm not happy about this at all. This is what I think of Coke and what it has done to this song...

[*He opens Coke. Pours the Coke on to the floor. As he talks the music grows louder and he has to match its volume. By the end he is screaming.*]

This song is about peace and love and harmony. It is not about Coke. Coke does not solve your problems. Coke does not stop wars. Coke does not unite people of all races across the hilly countryside every twenty years. Coke does nothing. NOTHING! NOW LISTEN TO THIS SONG ABOUT PEACE AND LOVE AND HARMONY! LISTEN!

[*He stares at the audience and begins to sing song. After a few beats he succumbs to the song and gets down on the floor and sucks up what he can of the Coke.*]

CURTAIN

# MAN IN THE STREETS

*[Robert sits on the stage floor with a magician's black hat and a section of newspaper. He one by one tears each page in half, crumpling it into a ball and placing the ball methodically on the stage eventually creating a circle of newspaper balls around him and then dismantling the circle by one by one picking them up and putting them in the hat.]*

**ROB:**

Hey, dead guy.
Hey dead guy,
  don't bring my day down.
I said,
Hey dead guy, don't bring my day down.
What are you, deaf?
You can't hear me from 'neath that light white police sheet?
Huh, dead guy, huh?

I don't want to see you.
I don't want to see you
   lying behind the NYU law library.
Not this early in the morning;
   not on my way to work.
I don't need to stop and stare,
    'Cause, dead guy, I'm late already.
Knowing I'll get that
   we-pay-you-don't-we look, when I get there,
   and the
   Nine-O'clock—We-said-9-to-6—Not-9:15-to-5:45—9-to-6
   lecture, again.

'Cause dead guy, it's Friday
   and I just wanted to cruise through the
      Fax this, call him, type that, Robert
      you wouldn't mind—game I play daily, unconscious.

'Cause dead guy, it's Friday
   and I just wanted to cruise through to the
      sleep sounds of Saturday morning,
      all curled up in a ball with Paula,
      just lazing in the bed til lunch pulls us out.

'Cause dead guy, it's Friday
   and I just wanted to make it
   without dealing with shit like this—
   shit that makes me stare at
      your dead ass prone from a shelterless stone cold slumber
   shit that makes me stare at
      your shit—
         a couple a bags a solitude,
         a crappy coat,
         somebody else's shoes
   shit that makes me stare at
      the New York City cop, thumbs tucked in his belt,
         leanin' against the bricks,
         thinkin' all maybe right with this morning—
         lusting after his horse . . .

   'Til he snaps out of it and comes at me with
      "Hey buddy, this ain't no freak show!'
      and he condescendingly taps his stick sharply between my eyes.

I stagger away;
   my eyes hurting like they've been eating ice cream too fast;
   my ears ringing from the canon ball blow to the head;
   and I hate the immediacy—the images caught in my memory.

I want forget you, dead guy, and your dead guy death.

I want to remember the Alamo.
'Cause those dead guys are long gone—
Only dead guys found in books.

And look I want to think 'Hey my worries and my shit are,
I don't know, significant.'
I want to know that something, some grand being
   gave more than two tosses when I was put here,
   and while we're at it—where that something is now?

Hey. . . are you two up there together?
Is that it, huh, dead guy? Already?
You two tossing with all the other dead guys
   laughing at me as I wander lost
      in the crowds that make the hour rush

laughing at me as I wander
the wrong way late away from work. Huh?
Is that the truth to report-not-so-live-man-in-the-streets,
huh, is it? The truth?

[*Robert picks up the hat and puts it on his head—with a cascade of newspaper balls.*]

CURTAIN

# A Trick of the Light

*[The following poem is delivered quietly (as if late at night), and a bit hypnotically at first, as if just coming out of the trance of absorption in the film just watched. The performer can be lit by the screen of a television set tuned to static; if another performer is available, he or she can hold the television and move it slowly around the monologuist to create an interesting lighting effect.]*

**DAVE:**
After the film is over you
sit very still almost as if
the flickering of the screen had
hypnotized you into believing
you were part of the film,
and now that the screen is blank
your mind is blank, your life is
empty and you are the ghost
of a ghost.

After the film is over you
sit unmoving dreaming of
the cornflake girl or the space commander
with the sky-blue eyes and when the
test pattern finally appears it's like hitting
the ground after a ten-year fall.

After the film the crabheaded spider-creature
asks you to dance and you offer it your arm
which it accepts, carefully, with one delicately
extended claw, you
trip over its many legs and it helps you up,
clicking and gurgling, asking you if you come
here often, if you know where to find
the traitor Delaunay.

After the film is over you wonder
why you've never been to Venice,
why you don't speak French better,
why you never answer letters. After the film
is over the telephone rings,
more faintly than usual, and just for a moment
you make believe you don't know who

it will be when you answer, it could be anyone,
anyone at all.

After the film is over you stare at the screen in
disbelief, surprised and vaguely offended that the
sense of story could desert you so easily,
leaving you stranded in a world without a coherent plot.
You examine your own life critically, looking for
character development and continuity and the emergence
of a really strong hero or two and maybe a magnificent
underlying theme to tie it all together,
but all you see are words on the page, the dance
of random dots.

After the film is over I notice
you've fallen asleep on my arm and I
want to wake you up so I can go to bed,
but it takes more than that to break
the silence at the end of the journey,
to shake off the spell of someone else's story
and find the courage to face your own.
Sometimes it takes until morning.
Sometimes it takes your whole life.

[*Blackout.*]

CURTAIN

# Eight Things She Doesn't Know

[*Blackout. Anita stands next to a five foot tall floor lamp which she clicks on. After each statement, she clicks the light off for a moment, then on again.*]

I accidentally dial her number thinking I'm dialing mine.

I lied to her about that thing in Mexico.

I'm sorry I didn't lie when she asked me if I liked that sculpture she kept on our mantle.

I wish I could visit the dog without calling first.

I wish she would visit the cats.

I keep that postcard on my desk.

I cook with lots and lots of onions now.

I miss her every day.

[*She clicks the lamp off.*]

CURTAIN

# Cats in the Cradle

© 1998 Anita Loomis

[*Anita holds a bright, yellow Beanie Baby cat up to her ear. She holds it to the ear of an audience member.*]

**ANITA:**
Can you hear that?

[*The audience member answers yes or no, usually no. Anita holds it to her ear again, then to another audience member.*]

Can you hear that?

[*The audience member answers. Anita listens some more and walks across the stage speaking.*]

I have three cats. I used to have four cats but one of them belonged to a lover and he shit on the bed. The cat, not the lover. So he had to go live at her mother's house. The lover's mother's, not the cat's mother's. I did have a lover who moved back to his mother's house, but that's different story. Actually, it isn't.

[*Anita lies down with her head propped up on the stage lip. She puts the cat on her belly and uses it as a puppet.*]

Every morning one of my three cats climbs up between my hips and starts to paw, paw, paw. Very exciting. Paw, paw, paw. We used to have sex in the morning. Me and my lover, not me and the cat. My lover would climb up between my hips and...

[*Anita looks at the clock or at the number of plays still hanging on the clothesline.*]

Ah, not enough time for details.

Sometimes, I get one cat on my stomach and one lying right on my breasts. A threesome.

When I get my period, my cats are furry heating pads.

One time I didn't get my period and my lover and I stopped having sex in the morning, or any time at all. My lover told me it was my decision, do whatever I wanted. We were standing in his mother's driveway. There were two of us standing there, not just me. So I asked him a question. He answered, "No, no I really don't."

[*Anita swings her body around and props her legs up as if in gyne-cological stirrups. She talks to the audience from this "upside down" position.*]

Lying on a cold bed with my legs spread for a complete stranger, I asked the nurse in the procedure room to turn off the radio. The doctor between my thighs said, "Oh, you won't even remember it."

Neil Diamond. The radio was playing Neil Diamond.

There was a poster tacked to the ceiling above my head.

[*Anita slowly floats the toy cat up above her, holding it in both hands.*]

It was a picture of a fuzzy, striped kitten in a miniature hot-air balloon. The caption read, "Dreams can take you anywhere." That was nine years, eleven months, twenty-seven days and one thousand, two hundred, and forty-eight miles from here.

[*Anita swings back around to her original position.*]

In the morning, one cat will sit on my belly, one on my chest and the third one on my shoulder, breathing gently in my ear like a sleeping lover.

[*She holds the cat to her ear again.*]

Can you hear that?

That's my biological clock.

It doesn't tick.

It purrs.

CURTAIN

# My MAP

© 2000 Lusia Strus

**LUSIA:**

His name is Michael Anthony Pastorello.

He has a dog named Vito.

Vito is a Shar-Pei.

Almost.

Mike got a deal.

He has all *The Sopranos* on tape.

That's how we started.

He made me go out to dinner with him in order to get the next 6 episodes.

I watched both seasons in two weeks.

I was a *Sopranos* whore.

My intention was to "hang out."

My intention was to sleep around for the summer.

He gave me this bracelet in a velvet box at Francesca's on Taylor Street. After gushing about how beautiful it was and what good taste it was in and I would have picked it out myself and I don't mean that as an insult but it's really beautiful...

He said, "It was the shiniest one."

And I said, "Oh my God. I'm in love with you."

He whispered, "Where have you been all my life?"

And I rolled over and, being 16 years younger than him, said, "In highschool!"

My parents were 16 years apart. It's fine.

We were walking past Linens 'n Things one day and I started doing something like this: [*Lusia makes high-pitched noises like an animal caught in a steel trap.*]

He asked me, "What's wrong?"

I managed to whisper that I just pictured us "registering" and what the hell was that all about?!

He said, "Yeah."

One day, after making him watch me do cartwheels in the backyard, I got on my knee, took his hand and said, "Michael Pastorello, you are the most beautiful, most genuinely kind and humble man I have ever known and I would be truly honored if you would be my bride."

He just stared at me and then said, "Get the fuck up."

He took me back to Francesca's last week.

And he gave me a tiny velvet box with something shiny in it.

And I said, "I love you."

My intention was to "hang out."

My intention was to sleep around for the summer.

Down the road, I pictured myself with...an assistant. Not a husband.

I thought that's the way I wanted to go.

And then it became very clear.

He's where I belong.

His name is Michael Anthony Pastorello.

And we almost have a Shar-Pei named Vito.

CURTAIN

# He's Story

*[A Fisher-Price™ plane is suspended from the ceiling, aimed at the floor. It's slowly lowered throughout this piece.]*

**PHIL:**

He's going down in flames now. His life is flashing before his eyes and he's not enjoying the show. One minute he's complaining about the in-flight movie, the next he's fumbling with his cell phone. Trying to think of who to call, who to tell how much he loves and how much he... nobody comes to mind. He was always selfish and that's how he's gonna go out: by himself. He thinks maybe if I were more generous with my wealth, but, silly man, when he says wealth he means money. He thinks if only I learned to love that person, but he forgets that he never learned how to love himself. Oh, he may have stopped to smell the roses every once in a while, but he never tasted one or planted one or gave one as a gift or painted one or... oh, he's going to die soon and well, honestly, what do we care? He's a tiny little man. Tiny enough to fit into a Fisher-Price™ airplane anyway. We know little men like him and we feel sorry for him, better than him, bigger than him. Yep, he's going down in flames now. His life is flashing before his eyes.

Aww, what the hell.

*[Phil grabs the airplane and sets it on a proper course.]*

I'm keeping my eye on you, little man.

CURTAIN

# Stonewalled,
# or The Sound of The Crowd

*[Dave sits on a chair stage right, in a shaft of light from extreme stage left that forms a square of light on the floor around his chair, suggesting the confines of a prison cell. The monologue is not delivered dramatically or angrily, but evenly, with quiet urgency and the slight suggestion of numbness.]*

**DAVE:**

I've always found something faintly horrifying about the sound of a large crowd cheering. It's one of the reasons I don't like sporting events, one of the reasons that those pep assemblies back in high school used to make my blood run cold. Even concerts do it to me sometimes, even when I love the band and want to cheer myself. Maybe it's because of all the atrocities that people around the world still gather in large groups to cheer—torture of humans and animals, floggings, bullfights, executions.

I think of the crowd that packed into a stadium in Afghanistan recently to watch three men be buried alive for committing what the law calls "sodomy." According to an Amnesty International report, the men were placed in front of a wall of stone, and while thousands of people watched, a tank drove into the wall and toppled it onto them. The men lay pinned under the rubble for half an hour. Two of them died the next day, the third is...believed to have survived. A month later two boys were bulldozed under a wall of dried mud. They were 18 and 22 years old, respectively.

I wonder at what age they began to feel sexual attraction to men. I wonder how long they struggled with their feelings before they finally reached out to touch another man, whether they understood as they reached out that the touch would mean lying mangled and suffocating under several tons of mud. Whether they heard, from somewhere, the sinister sound of cheering carried faintly on the wind.

I wonder what they think about as they wait to die. I imagine that on a warm spring night like tonight, as countless cocktails are being raised in the bars along Halsted Street, as men are touching freely in the dark corners of Man's Country or the Unicorn, and I sit here on stage as an open—or as they used to say when I was growing up, "avowed"—

**185**

homosexual, at the very same moment an 18 year-old boy is sitting in a cell or dungeon somewhere, knowing that within 24 hours he'll learn what it's like to have a wall of rocks collapse on him. And, if he survives the initial impact, to lie pinned underneath it, crushed and bleeding. While no one comes to help him. While thousands cheer.

[*Blackout.*]

CURTAIN

# Grins and Saltwater

[*A tight spotlight. John is in a chair center stage. He is holding a very small novelty laugh box. It is barely perceptible to the audience.*]

**JOHN:**

Comedy and Tragedy walk into a bar. Tragedy approaches the bartender and says: "I'll have a bottle of vodka and one shot glass."

The bartender turns to Comedy and asks if he wants anything. Comedy replies: "No thank you. I'm just here to cheer him up."

[*He presses the little button to make the laugh box sound its sound. He has a deadpan expression. After the laughing has stopped, a short pause before continuing.*]

A while later, Tragedy's pale, sweaty face is pressed against the top of the bar. He's pouring vodka into the corner of his mouth and whimpering to himself. The bartender turns to Comedy and remarks:

"I thought you said you were here to cheer him up?" Comedy replies:

"I thought so too, but maybe I'm just laughing at him." [*Pause.*] "Sometimes it's hard to tell."

[*Laugh box. Lights fade.*]

CURTAIN

# A Single Minute Out Of Fifty-Six Hundred Consecutive Minutes In The Mind

[*Blackout. Sean sits center stage. A spot comes up on him.*]

**SEAN:**

I like the word. It's a nice word. A new word. It's not a new word. It's a new word to me.

[*A recording of Sean repeating the word "acromioclavicular" begins, and continues as Sean speaks. At first he can speak over it but it eventually drowns him out.*]

I like the way it sounds. It flows off the tongue. I like saying it. I had never heard it before. I have heard the abbreviation, which is AC joint. It's where the clavicle meets the acromion. Since I have heard the word it has been stuck in my head. It's like a song that you hear and can't get out of your head. Like Billy Idol's "Flesh for Fantasy." I don't know any other words so just that little part is stuck in my head. I can feel it right here above my eye, drilling deeper and deeper into my head. It takes over everything. No thoughts are possible. Nothing gets done inside my head. I can't plan or think or clear my mind or relax. It is always there. Acromioclavicular. [*Recording stops.*] I said it out loud at the bus stop to make it stop in my head.

[*There is silence for about ten seconds and then recording resumes. Lights fade out.*]

CURTAIN

# Branded

words and music by
Genevra Gallo

Some - time___ last___ year___ I'm hav - ing___ din -
ner___ with___ my___ dad___ and he says, "My___ dear,___ it's clear that
you're in love___ and___ for that I am___ glad. But we should have___ seen___
_ you___ walk - ing down___ the___ wed - ding aisle___ by now."___
_ And he ut - ters this in - sult - ing met - a - phor___ in___
which I am a cow: Why___ buy...___ Why___
buy...___ Why___ buy___ the___ cow when you can
get the milk___ for___ free? Then my___ mom
sends me an___ e - mail the oth - er___ day, "No - thing___

# Tiny Satan

words and music by
Anita Loomis

Verse 1:
When Sa-tan was a ti-ny ba-by, Sa-tan had no friends.

His mo-ther left him all a-lone Stuck in a play-pen. Oh!

Chorus:
Ti - ny Sa-tan all a-lone, Ti - ny Sa-tan

ba - - - by. Ti - ny Sa-tan all a-lone,

soon you will be ha - ting. Ba-dum-dum-bum!

Verse 2:
When Sa-tan was a pid-dee lad his lit-tle life was hard.

(repeat chorus)
His pa-rents made him go and play a-lone in the back-yard. Oh!

Verse 3:
Just as Sa-tan went out-side the rain came in a flood. WHOOSH!

Ti - ny Sa-tan slip and slide fell down in the mud.

**192**

# Index by Title

# Index by Author

**198**

# The Ensemble

For a history of The Neo-Futurists and a more detailed account of the workings of *Too Much Light Makes The Baby Go Blind,* I refer you to our first book *100 Neo-Futurist Plays from Too Much Light Makes The Baby Go Blind* and to the company's Web site (www.neofuturists.org).

### The Neo-Futurists, in order of appearance in *Too Much Light*:

| | |
|---|---|
| Greg Allen* | Scott Hermes |
| Randy Burgess | Diana Slickman |
| Phil Gibbs | Lusia Strus |
| Rex Jenny | David Kodeski |
| Kathy Keyes | Anita Loomis |
| Melissa Lindberg | Stephanie Shaw |
| Robin MacDuffie | Bill Coelius |
| Mike Troccoli | Rob Neill |
| Sheri Reda | Steve Mosqueda* |
| Karen Christopher | Rachel Claff* |
| Lisa Buscani | Sean Benjamin* |
| Alexis Smith | Geryll Robinson |
| Phil Ridarelli | John Pierson* |
| Ted Bales | Rachelle Anthes |
| Adrian Danzig | Noelle Krimm* |
| Ayun Halliday | Marjorie Fitzsimmons |
| Page Phillips | Connor Kalista |
| Dave Awl | Andy Bayiates* |
| Spencer Kayden | Genevra Gallo* |
| Heather Riordan* | Chloë Johnston* |
| Betsy Freytag | Ryan Walters* |
| Tim Rienhard | Jason Torrence* |
| Greg Kotis | Joe Dempsey* |

*Current *Too Much Light* ensemble as of August, 2002.

## ACKNOWLEDGMENTS

Thanks to all The Neo-Futurists involved for their patience, real or assumed, on the long road to the completion of this book. Particular thanks are due to those who helped me with editorial tasks: Dave Awl, Anita Loomis, Ayun Halliday, Connor Kalista, David Kodeski, John Pierson, Louise Molnar and Kristen Swann. Louise Molnar's design is a thing of beauty for which I am also grateful. Many thanks to Jeff Kowalkowski and Christopher Gurr for their musical transcription work. And finally, I am indebted to President Bob Stockfish for taking time out of his busy Sunday morning to help.

D.S.

# ALSO AVAILABLE FROM HOPE AND NONTHINGS

**H&N001    INCOMPLETE PHILOSOPHY OF HOPE AND NONTHINGS**
ian pierce / Selected plays by Neo-Futurist John Pierson,
a.k.a. ian pierce.                                                    $10.00

**H&N002    HALF LI(V)ES**
Anita Loomis / Stories, poems, and monologues.              $8.00

**H&N003    LIKE HELL**
Ben Weasel / A punk rock novel.                             $12.00

**H&N004    DEVOLUTION**
Sean Benjamin / A play of 40 scenes in random order.        $8.00
                                        (Available late 2002.)

**H&N005    AN APOLOGY FOR THE COURSE AND OUTCOME
            OF CERTAIN EVENTS DELIVERED BY DOCTOR JOHN FAUSTUS
            ON THIS HIS FINAL EVENING & THE HUNCHBACK VARIATIONS**
Mickle Maher / Two one-act plays by Chicago playwright &
Theater Oobleck co-founder, Mickle Maher.                   $10.00

**H&N006    WEASELS IN A BOX: A NOT SO MUSICAL JOURNEY
            THROUGH PARTIALLY TRUTHFUL SITUATIONS WITH
            EIGHTY PERCENT FICTITIOUS DIALOGUE.**
John R. Pierson-Jughead-ian pierce / A punk rock novel.     $12.00
        (Contact Hope and Nonthings for release date and more info.)

**H&N008    PUNK IS A FOUR-LETTER WORD**
Ben Weasel / Collected essays from a punk rock journalist.
Includes previously unpublished material.                   $12.00

**H&N009    WHAT THE SEA MEANS: POEMS, STORIES & MONOLOGUES
            1987-2002**
Dave Awl / The first book collection of work by writer-performer
Dave Awl, poet, Neo-Futurist, founder of The Pansy Kings
and "surrealist insomniac mystic."                          $12.00

These books can be ordered through mail.
Hope And Nonthings / P.O. Box 148010 / Chicago, IL 60614-8010
(Add $1.50 postage per item. $2.50 Overseas)
Check or Money order made out to: Hope And Nonthings
www.hopeandnonthings.com  (for other purchasing information)